LEGENDS OF WARFARE

NAVAL

USS Alabama (BB-60)

From Tarawa, Leyte Gulf, and Okinawa, to Museum Ship

DAVID DOYLE

SCHIFFER MILITARY

4880 Lower Valley Road   Atglen, PA 19310

Designed by Justin Watkinson
Type set in Impact/Minion Pro/Univers LT Std

ISBN: 978-0-7643-6235-4
Printed in China

Published by Schiffer Publishing, Ltd.
4880 Lower Valley Road
Atglen, PA 19310
Phone: (610) 593-1777; Fax: (610) 593-2002
E-mail: Info@schifferbooks.com
www.schifferbooks.com

For our complete selection of fine books on this and related subjects, please visit our website at www.schifferbooks.com. You may also write for a free catalog.

Schiffer Publishing's titles are available at special discounts for bulk purchases for sales promotions or premiums. Special editions, including personalized covers, corporate imprints, and excerpts, can be created in large quantities for special needs. For more information, contact the publisher.

We are always looking for people to write books on new and related subjects. If you have an idea for a book, please contact us at proposals@schifferbooks.com.

Acknowledgments

The materials contained in these pages were compiled from the records of the Norfolk Naval Shipyard, the Puget Sound Naval Shipyard, the Naval History and Heritage Command, the Battleship USS *Alabama* Memorial Park, the National Museum of Naval Aviation, the Mariners Museum, and the National Archives and Records Administration.

In compiling this history I was truly blessed to have the invaluable help of many colleagues that I am fortunate to call my friends, including Tom Kailbourn, Scott Taylor, A. D. Baker III, James Noblin, Sean Hert, Tracy White, Rick Davis, Jerry Leslie, Roger Torgeson, and Dana Bell. Their generous and skillful assistance adds immensely to the quality of this volume. I am especially blessed to have the ongoing help of my wonderful wife, Denise, who has scanned thousands of photos and documents for this and numerous other books. Beyond that, she is an ongoing source of support and inspiration.

All photos are from the collections of the US National Archives and Records Administration unless otherwise noted.

Contents

Introduction   004

CHAPTER 1   Construction   006

CHAPTER 2   Commissioning and Fleet Service   018

CHAPTER 3   Memorial   059

Introduction

USS *Alabama* and her three sister ships, *South Dakota, Indiana,* and *Massachusetts,* together make up the next-to-the-last group of US Navy battleships—the South Dakota class. Only the battlewagons of the Iowa class are of more recent make. It was in March 1937 that design work began on *Alabama* and the other South Dakota–class vessels—all of them "treaty battleships" (i.e., vessels that conformed to the requirements of the naval treaties concluded among the world's great maritime powers). These agreements restricted battleship displacement to 35,000 tons and limited the warships' guns to a maximum 16-inch bore. It was the US's standard practice for a battleship's armor to be designed to protect it from an equally armed opponent. This meant, as far as the South Dakota battleships were concerned, that they would have sufficient armor to withstand gunfire from an enemy's 16-inch guns. To armor a battleship to that degree without exceeding the overall 35,000-ton displacement limit meant that the vessel had to be relatively short and compact. *Alabama*'s length fell just under 680 feet, giving the ship a stubby configuration, the shape of its hull less than ideal and the room aboard her for engineering spaces limited. Because of these treaty limitations, *Alabama* had a top speed of 27.8 knots or 32 miles per hour.

War was already raging in Asia and Europe when the laying of *Alabama*'s keel on February 1, 1940, kicked off the ship's construction at Norfolk Navy Yard. Engineers and draftsmen by the score refined the design of the battleship. Hastened by the Japanese attack on Pearl Harbor, droves of shipyard workers laboring almost around the clock constructed her from the keel up. She was launched on February 16, 1942, nine months ahead of the original schedule. The accelerated pace of construction continued through the fitting-out period. Typically, when a warship is launched, she is little more than a hull, with some of the machinery in place. In exactly six months of round-the-clock labor, shipyard workers turned the floating hull into a finished battleship, and on August 16, 1942, *Alabama* was commissioned.

Specifications		
Length overall		679 ft., 5⁵⁄₁₆ in.
Length at waterline		666 ft., 0 in.
Maximum beam		107 ft., 11 in.
Waterline beam		108 ft., 1½ in.
Mean draft		33 ft., 9¹³⁄₁₆ in. @ 42,545 tons
Maximum draft		36 ft., 2 in.
Displacement		39,892 tons, standard
		44,500 tons, full load, 1942
Machinery	Boilers	Eight Foster Wheeler
	Geared turbines	Four sets Westinghouse, 130,000 shaft horsepower forward, 32,000 astern
Speed		27.8 knots
Complement 1945		2,332 (127 officers, 2,205 enlisted)
Cost		Approximately $80 million

An Illinois-class pre-dreadnaught-type battleship, USS *Alabama* (BB-8) was launched in May 1898. Displacing 11,565 tons and armed with a main battery of four 13-inch/35-caliber guns mounted in two turrets, BB-8 was the second warship commissioned by the US Navy with the name *Alabama. Library of Congress*

Decommissioned on May 7, 1920, USS *Alabama* was handed over to the War Department to be used as a target ship on September 15, 1921. After being targeted by US Army Air Service bombs in late September 1925, the former member of Teddy Roosevelt's Great White Fleet is seen here, sunk in the Chesapeake Bay's shallow waters. *National Museum of Naval Aviation*

CHAPTER 1
Construction

On February 1, 1940, dignitaries and spectators convened at the Norfolk Navy Yard in Portsmouth, Virginia, for the keel-laying ceremony for the second US battleship *Alabama* (BB-60). The traditional ceremony for the laying of a ship's keel marked the official start of the vessel's construction. *Battleship USS Alabama Memorial Park*

Design work on *Alabama* got underway nearly three years before the ship's keel laying on February 1, 1940. It was in March 1937 that designers began to set down the characteristics of "Battleship 1939," the new design that was slated for fiscal year 1939, which, in terms of the regular calendar, started on July 1, 1938. After receiving approval on January 4, 1938, the characteristics would elicit congressional appropriation for two such battleships on April 4, 1938. These first two vessels—of the group destined to become the South Dakota class—were *South Dakota* (BB-57) and *Indiana* (BB-58). Tension around the world was escalating steadily, however. Japanese forces continued their rapid advance deep into China, having occupied the Chinese capital at the end of the previous year. Meanwhile in Europe, Germany's annexation of Austria in March 1938 led not to relaxation but to a new and greater crisis over Czechoslovakia, which dominated headlines that spring and summer. In light of such world developments, it is unsurprising that the US Congress moved to authorize construction of two more South Dakota–class battleships—*Massachusetts* (BB-59) and *Alabama* (BB-60) on June 25, 1938.

In the aftermath of World War I, there had been considerable international optimism about the prospect of avoiding another global war by limiting the size and effectiveness of warships. The major maritime powers were able to agree on a series of naval treaties that restricted ships' armament and size. But by the mid-1930s, international tensions had risen to such a degree that the naval treaty system was beginning to unravel. Built, nevertheless, within the treaty limits, South Dakota–class ships had limited space and were somewhat vulnerable to torpedoes. All four battleships underwent construction at about the same time. New York Shipbuilding Company constructed *South Dakota*, Bethlehem Shipbuilding built *Massachusetts*, Newport News Shipbuilding and Drydock Company

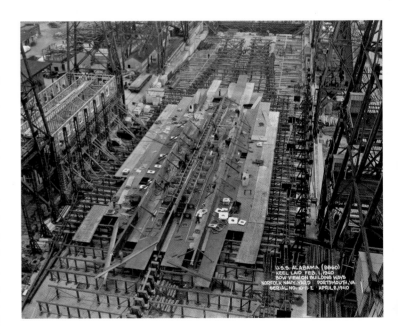

The bottom of *Alabama*'s hull can be seen coming together in this April 2, 1940, view, facing aft from over the bow. Already in place are the plates that form the shell—the outer skin—of the ship's hull. The keel is being constructed atop those plates, which are known as strakes. *Norfolk Naval Shipyard*

Further progress in the construction of *Alabama* is seen in this June 28, 1940, view from the ship's stem looking forward. Assembly of the keel and the perforated lateral frame sections proceeds amidships. Installation has also begun of the curved shell plates to the sides of the bottom of the hull. Holding the shell plates are supports with curved cradles. Eventually, the frame of the ship will be extended and fastened to the plates, once a sufficient number of shell plates have been fitted together. *National Archives*

Lateral bulkheads for machinery spaces are in the background in this view from above *Alabama*'s stern on September 27, 1940. Below the gangway to the left in the foreground are the curved shell plates that are part of the tunnel stern—a recess in the bottom of the stern located between the outboard propellers. This feature allowed for greater hull volume toward the stern and made it harder for a single torpedo blast to take out all four of the propellers. *National Archives*

produced *Indiana,* and *Alabama* was built at the nearby Norfolk Navy Yard. After the Japanese attack on Pearl Harbor brought war to the United States, the more than 3,000 construction workers labored on *Alabama* with even-greater determination.

Two months into the war, *Alabama*'s hull was complete and dignitaries assembled one morning to hear Navy secretary Frank Knox give a speech and to watch Mrs. Lister Hill christen the ship. At 1030 on February 16, 1942, *Alabama* was formally launched. Although the hull was now named and afloat, a great deal more work remained before she would be a completed battleship.

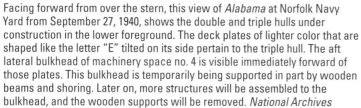

Facing forward from over the stern, this view of *Alabama* at Norfolk Navy Yard from September 27, 1940, shows the double and triple hulls under construction in the lower foreground. The deck plates of lighter color that are shaped like the letter "E" tilted on its side pertain to the triple hull. The aft lateral bulkhead of machinery space no. 4 is visible immediately forward of those plates. This bulkhead is temporarily being supported in part by wooden beams and shoring. Later on, more structures will be assembled to the bulkhead, and the wooden supports will be removed. *National Archives*

"Merry Christmas and a Happy New Year" proclaims a small sign on the top front of the barbette of turret 2 on December 30, 1940. A drawing of three wise men riding camels completes the holiday greeting. Aft of the barbette on the deck is a Christmas tree. The circular opening at the top of the barbette of turret 3 can be seen in the background. The ladders for the workmen are made of wood and built double wide so as to allow for two workers to occupy the same level at the same time. *Battleship USS Alabama Memorial Park*

In another Christmas season view from December 30, 1940, the hull is surveyed from above the stern and somewhat to the left of the vantage point of the preceding photo. A dense network of scaffolds were assembled on the sides of the hull along the building ways. Called staging, the scaffolds rose higher and higher in keeping with the work on the growing structure of the ship. Towers for large, track-mounted overhead cranes are visible to the far left and in the right background. Large, heavy ship assemblies were hauled into their proper positions by means of the overhead cranes. *National Archives*

The forward bulkhead of the citadel is visible to the front of barbette 1 in this close-up view of *Alabama*'s forward section on July 1, 1941. The citadel, the sides of which were the belt armor, was the armored structure that protected the vital belowdecks spaces. The citadel's forward bulkhead was 11.3-inch class A armor. *National Archives*

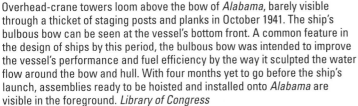

Overhead-crane towers loom above the bow of *Alabama*, barely visible through a thicket of staging posts and planks in October 1941. The ship's bulbous bow can be seen at the vessel's bottom front. A common feature in the design of ships by this period, the bulbous bow was intended to improve the vessel's performance and fuel efficiency by the way it sculpted the water flow around the bow and hull. With four months yet to go before the ship's launch, assemblies ready to be hoisted and installed onto *Alabama* are visible in the foreground. *Library of Congress*

With its gunhouse floor atop the pan-floor assembly, this is the turret 2 assembly as it looked on December 18, 1941. Here a crane is transferring the assembly from the Norfolk Navy Yard's turret shop to the location where the electric deck will be attached below the pan floor. Also called the machinery floor, the electric deck contained electric-hydraulic machinery for operating the turret, and the stations for the three gun layers and the turret trainer who set the elevation of the 16-inch guns and the turret's train. *Norfolk Navy Yard*

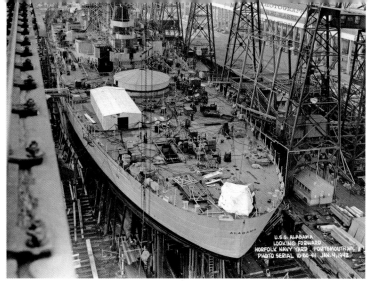

A temporary shelter has been installed on the deck aft of turret 3's barbette. Visible to the lower bottom of the hull, in this January 4, 1942, view from the stern, is the skeg and shaft of the outboard port propeller. The ship's smokestack is enveloped in staging. *Battleship USS Alabama Memorial Park*

Temporary weatherproof covers are installed over *Alabama*'s main-battery barbettes on Sunday, January 4, 1942—four weeks to the day after Pearl Harbor and six weeks before the launch of the ship. Near the bow at the bottom of the hull, the fore poppet is under construction. A part of the cradle, the fore poppet was a temporary structure that was built in the run-up to launch. Its purpose was to transfer the ship's weight from the building ways onto the sliding ways, along which the vessel would glide into the water when it was launched. *Battleship USS Alabama Memorial Park*

Wooden props referred to as shores support and stabilize the stern of the Alabama on the day preceding launching. The removal of the shores under the stern was one of the earliest steps in the launching operation, beginning about 90 minutes after the start of the operation. *Battleship USS Alabama Memorial Park*

U.S.S. ALABAMA (BB60)
CHRISTENING OF VESSEL
SPONSOR - MRS. LISTER HILL
NORFOLK NAVY YARD   PORTSMOUTH, VA.
PHOTO SERIAL 10-104   FEB. 16, 1942

Under the gaze of assembled dignitaries, *Alabama*'s sponsor, Mrs. Henrietta Hill, smashes the traditional champagne bottle on the battleship's bow, christening the vessel. According to naval tradition, a ship's good fortune requires that it be christened with champagne or possibly some other wine when it is launched. *Battleship USS Alabama Memorial Park*

Seen from the center of the ways as she glides toward the water, *Alabama* is finally launched. A large grid has been painted on the bow's starboard side, and a line has been painted in a light color on the boot topping: the black band that surrounds the ship and extends above and below the waterline. It is unclear what the purpose of the grid and the light-colored line was. These features were applied only to the starboard side of the hull. Several passengers can be seen standing on staging planks high over the main deck. *Naval History and Heritage Command*

Converging on *Alabama*, seen here from the starboard side, tugboats will move the ship to the fitting-out dock. A good deal of work remains to complete the ship, but already much of the superstructure is present, including the conning tower at the forward part of the ship and the aft fire-control tower toward the rear. *Naval History and Heritage Command*

Staging for work parties surrounds *Alabama*'s superstructure and hangs down along her hull as she undergoes fitting-out at the Norfolk Navy Yard on April 2, 1942, six weeks after her launch. Still visible here, the boot topping—the black stripe that surrounds the hull and marks the eventual water line—will sink beneath the waves when the ship is complete and additional weight has been added to the vessel. *Norfolk Naval Shipyard*

The weldment for turret number 1 is lowered into its barbette on *Alabama* on April 26, 1942. Making up the weldment are, *top to bottom*, the lateral bulkhead that divides the turret officer's booth from the gun compartments, the gunhouse floor, the pan floor, and, at the bottom, the electric deck. Visible in this view are the door openings in the lateral bulkhead that will offer access to the three gun compartments and to the compartments for the right and left sight pointers and sight trainers. There is a temporary cover over the barbette for turret number 2 in the foreground. *Norfolk Naval Shipyard*

Now, almost four months since *Alabama* was launched and with about two months remaining before her commissioning, the fitting-out is well advanced. The date is June 8, 1942, and the main-battery turrets are under construction. The faceplate on the turret number 1 gunhouse is in place but has yet to be installed on turret 2. Also not yet installed are the 16-inch/45-caliber guns. Above and aft of turret 2 is the dark shape of the conning tower. Visible above and aft of the conning tower are the superstructure's upper forward levels, which are sometimes called the foretop or forward tower. *Battleship USS Alabama Memorial Park*

U.S.S. Alabama (BB60)
Stern View at Fitting Out Berth
Norfolk Navy Yard Portsmouth, Va.
Photo Serial 10-172-48 July 3, 1942

Workmen continue fitting out *Alabama* on July 3, 1942, in this view of the ship from the stern. Temporary shelters and materials and assemblies can be seen set up and laid out on the deck. Tubs for quadruple (quad) 40 mm antiaircraft gun mounts can be seen on the fantail and overhanging it. Next to each of the tubs for the quad mounts is a raised tub of smaller size. This is intended for the director of the adjacent 40 mm gun mount. Its boom lowered, the aircraft crane is visible between the gun tubs. The gunhouse of turret 3, seen farther forward on the ship, still lacks frontal armor and the major part of its roof. Inside the gunhouse, trunnion cradles for the 16-inch guns can be discerned. *Battleship USS Alabama Memorial Park*

This July 3, 1942, view of *Alabama* from above reveals numerous details of the vessel. The wildcats, by which the anchor chain was raised and lowered by the windlass, are visible at lower left. The breakwater, a bulwark that diverted any waves that might splash over the forecastle, is seen aft of the wildcats. Lying on the main deck, aft of the breakwater's starboard edge is a paravane, an antimine "glider" device that would be towed alongside the ship. Although the 5-inch gun mounts are installed, their gunhouses are still missing. Accordingly, canvas covers have been fitted over the gun mounts. *National Archives*

U.S.S. ALABAMA (BB60)
BOW VIEW AT FITTING OUT BERTH
NORFOLK NAVY YARD PORTSMOUTH VA.
PHOTO SERIAL 10-174-50 JULY 3, 1942

CHAPTER 2
Commissioning and Fleet Service

Much of the vessel's superstructure, most of her interior fittings, and all of her powerful guns had yet to be put in place. Typically, when a warship is launched, she is little more than a hull, with some of the machinery in place. The superstructure, guns, galley equipment, communications equipment, and, in the case of *Alabama*, the hull armor, as well as literally tens of thousands of other items required to creating a functional, livable, seagoing, and combat-ready vessel, are installed during the fitting-out period. As a result of these efforts *Alabama* was placed into commission on August 16, 1942, only six months after the launching. With the crew at last brought aboard, the naval vessel came to life.

After months of training and drills as the crew became familiar with their new ship, *Alabama* departed Norfolk Navy Yard on November 11, 1942, and embarked on a shakedown and training period in Chesapeake Bay that was to last four months. She headed to Casco Bay off Portland, Maine, and then sailed back to Chesapeake Bay on January 11. She returned to Norfolk Navy Yard for a refit that involved strengthening the ship's antiaircraft defenses and saw to replacing her mottled Measure 12 camouflage with the camouflage scheme known as Measure 22, which was a graded system of 5-N Navy Blue with 5-H Haze Gray. This scheme provided for Navy Blue to extend up from the waterline to a horizontal line even with the lowest point of the edge of the main deck. Upward from there, the ship's vertical surfaces were painted Haze Gray. Horizontal surfaces were painted—not stained—Deck Blue.

Following the refit, *Alabama* once again set off for Casco Bay, where she arrived on February 13, 1943, and joined Task Group 22.2. Then, as a part of Task Force 22, together with *South Dakota*, her sister ship and leader of her class, and behind a screen of five destroyers, she turned toward the Orkney Islands on April 2, 1943. Passing Newfoundland, *Alabama* reached Scapa Flow on May 19, 1943, and joined Task Force 61, becoming part of the British Home Fleet. In this capacity, her role was to reinforce the Royal Navy's convoy support forces. In order to provide cover for the reinforcement of Spitzbergen, *Alabama* crossed the Arctic Circle in June, her crew becoming duly certified "bluenoses" for their cruise to the far north.

In July, *Alabama* was involved in Operation Governor off Norway, a diversion to draw attention away from the landings in Sicily as well as an effort to draw *Tirpitz* and *Scharnhorst* into a battle with the superior Allied force. While the Germans did not take the bait and instead remained in Altafjord, the effect was that the bulk of the German surface fleet was pinned down.

Alabama, along with her sister ship *South Dakota*, was detached from the British Home Fleet for return to the United States on August 1, 1943. The battleships arrived at Norfolk Navy Yard on August 9, with *Alabama* entering the yard for overhaul prior to being dispatched to the Pacific. The shipyard work was completed, with *Alabama* steaming for the Pacific on August 20, passing through the Panama Canal on August 25 and reaching New Hebrides on September 14. There she would remain for six weeks, during which time the crew continued to drill.

On November 7, *Alabama* steamed for Fiji, then four days later sailed to take part in the Gilbert and Marshall Islands campaign by providing antiaircraft screening for the fast aircraft carriers.

The battleship finally used her 16-inch rifles in combat when she along with five other US Navy fast battleships shelled Japanese installations on the island of Nauru on December 8. USS *Alabama* fired 535 16-inch rounds at enemy installations on Nauru. While *Alabama* was unscathed in this action, the destroyer *Boyd* (DD-544) was struck by Japanese artillery and came alongside *Alabama* to transfer three wounded men aboard the battleship, which had superior medical facilities.

At last the day has come for *Alabama* to be commissioned. Members of the crew and some civilians have begun gathering on the quarterdeck on August 16, 1942, for the ceremonies during which the US Navy would formally take possession of the battleship, whose name would then be preceded by the official designation "United States Ship" (USS). *Alabama* was painted in Measure 12 (Modified) camouflage, with patterns in Navy Blue (5-N), Ocean Gray (5-O), and Haze Gray 5-H) painted on vertical surfaces, and Deck Blue on the decks. Even now, during commissioning, turret 3's roof remains incomplete. *Battleship USS Alabama Memorial Park*

As a part of her commissioning, USS *Alabama* formally received her first commander, Capt. George B. Wilson, who read his orders, took command of the vessel, and then set the first watch. In keeping with tradition, Capt. Wilson gave the crew their first order to "Man our ship and bring her to life." *Battleship USS Alabama Memorial Park*

Alabama retired to Efate, arriving on December 12, 1943. She steamed for the shipyard at Pearl Harbor January 5, 1944, arriving January 12. There she had her port outboard propeller replaced, as well as undergoing routine maintenance.

Steaming once again toward Japan, *Alabama* arrived at Funafuti in the Ellice Islands on January 21. Assigned to Task Group (TG) 58.2, she left on January 25 to take part in Operation Flintlock, the invasion of Kwajalein. Along with *South Dakota* and *North Carolina*, *Alabama* bombarded Roi-Namur on January 29–30. During this action *Alabama* expended 330 16-inch and 1,562 5-inch rounds, destroying enemy aircraft, gun emplacements, and buildings.

On February 12, 1944, *Alabama* steamed toward Truk from Kwajalein in concert with Task Group 58.2, including USS *Bunker Hill*. In what was dubbed Operation Hailstone, *Alabama*'s role was that of a massive antiaircraft battery, intent on defending the carriers. Aircraft from TG58.2 struck the island on February 16–17, causing substantial damage.

From Truk, *Alabama* and TG58.2 steamed toward the Marianas to assist in strikes on Tinian, Saipan, and Guam. On February 21, 1944, while en route to the Marianas and under Japanese air attack, a fatal incident took place. Like other US battleships, *Alabama* was built with firing locks that prevented the secondary batteries' 5-inch guns from shooting into their own ship. *Alabama* was operating as a part of Task Group 58.2 when it came under air attack on February 21–22. As the ship was turning toward the right, the mounts were also swinging as they tracked the enemy target. Soon, however, they hit the limit of their swing as fixed by the firing lock. Thinking the firing line to be clear, the mount 9 sight setter believed the lock had malfunctioned and overrode the safety feature. Mount 9's right gun unleashed an AA common round that blasted into the high center of mount 5's rear plate and detonated inside the gun compartment. A second antiaircraft round fired by mount 9's left gun nicked mount 5's left edge and exploded outside that mount.

All thirteen crewmen in mount 5 were injured. The scalp and lower extremities were all that remained of the mount captain. Bone fragments from the mount captain inflicted injuries on a Mount 5 crewmate. Outside the mount, a steward's mate who had left his battle station in the clipping room was killed. Shell fragments wounded two signalmen on the signal bridge. The blast ruptured the eardrums of three men at quad #2. At sunset the next day, *Alabama* buried her five dead at sea in a ceremony led jointly by Catholic and Protestant chaplains.

Despite the incident, *Alabama* continued her sweep southeast of Saipan, then steamed with the task group to Majuro on February 26 for refueling and taking aboard ammunition.

Alabama and Task Group 58.3 steamed from Majuro on March 22, 1944, with USS *Yorktown* (CV-10) at center, bound for Palau, Yap, Ulithi, and Woleai, Caroline Islands. The force came under attack on the night of March 29, with four ships in *Alabama*'s area coming under attack, one of which was downed by the battleship's gunners. The next day, as the carrier launched its airstrikes, another enemy aircraft approached the warships but was driven off by antiaircraft fire before it could press home its attack.

After a brief respite at Majuro, *Alabama* sailed with USS *Enterprise* (CV-6) on April 13, striking enemy targets on Hollandia, Wakde, Sawar, and Sarmi along the New Guinea coast, as well as covering Army landings at Aitape, Tanahmerah Bay, and Humboldt Bay, and launching further strikes on Truk, all within a three-week period. At the close of this time, *Alabama* along with five other fast battleships shelled Ponape on May 1, with *Alabama* firing for seventy minutes.

May 4, 1944, found *Alabama* at Eniwetok for a month of training and repair, getting underway once again as part of Operation Forager, the US effort to capture islands close enough to Japan to use as bases for B-29 raids on Japan. On June 13, *Alabama* shelled the west coast of Saipan for six hours.

The Battle of the Philippine Sea was intended to be the Japanese all-out effort to destroy the US Navy fast-carrier task force, inflicting such losses of personnel that a negotiated peace be sought, rather than unconditional surrender. On June 19, at 1006, *Alabama*'s radar picked up the approaching Japanese aircraft, the first ship in the US fleet to do so. US carrier-borne aircraft went aloft to defend the fleet, the result of which became known as the Marianas Turkey Shoot, with Japanese losses totaling 433 carrier aircraft, along with three aircraft carriers, and about 200 land-based aircraft destroyed. US losses were 134 aircraft, eighty of which were lost when they ran out of fuel, although most of the crews were recovered. During this action, *Alabama*'s antiaircraft defenses fired on multiple aircraft, and one Japanese aircraft dropped two small bombs near the ship.

After further screening the US landing force on Saipan, *Alabama* withdrew to the Marshalls for maintenance. Sailing as flagship Battleship Division 9, *Alabama* left Eniwetok on July 14, 1944, screening a task group built around USS *Bunker Hill* striking Guam in support of the landing of July 21. Again retiring to Eniwetok, she was next underway along with USS *Essex* (CV-9) as part of Operation "Stalemate II," the seizure of Palau, Ulithi, and Yap. Following strikes on the Carolines on September 6 through 9, *Alabama* steamed to the Philippines to shield the carriers striking the islands of Cebu, Leyte, Bohol, and Negros on September 12–14; Manila Bay on September 21 and 22; and the central Philippines on September 24.

USS *Alabama* underwent more work and completed trials in the waters off Norfolk, Virginia, after her commissioning. On November 11, 1942, she was ready for actual sea trials in Chesapeake Bay and the Atlantic Ocean. Then, a few weeks later, she was performing a shakedown run when an aircraft from Hampton Roads Naval Air Station caught this view of her. Snow and ice can be seen on the decks and other surfaces of the ship. Stowed atop the turret roofs are life rafts. Also visible is the rectangular opening of the smokestack. *National Archives*

After a brief stop in Saipan on September 28, *Alabama* steamed to Ulithi on October 1. On October 6, *Alabama* again steamed with the fast-carrier task group as TF 38 struck Okinawa, then moved on to Luzon on October 14. During this action, *Alabama*'s antiaircraft batteries claimed three Japanese aircraft downed and a fourth damaged. October 15 found *Alabama* supporting landing operations on Leyte.

The now-veteran battleship continued her role screening aircraft carriers, first during strikes on Cebu, Negros, Panay, northern Mindanao, and Leyte on October 21, 1944, then against the Japanese Southern Force in the area off Suriago Strait.

After having received reports of a Japanese fleet on the move, the fast-carrier task force, including *Alabama*, steamed for Cape Engano, while on October 24, despite losing four carriers, the Japanese force passed through the San Bernardino Strait, to attack a task group made up of American escort carriers, destroyers, and destroyer escorts. *Alabama* and her company reversed course, discarding Cape Engano and racing toward the Japanese fleet attacking the escort carriers. Unfortunately, the Japanese had withdrawn by the time the US reinforcements had arrived. After providing escort for *Essex* a bit longer, *Alabama* retired to Ulithi on October 30 for replenishment. For most of November, *Alabama* steamed with the fast carriers as they struck Luzon and Visayas, returning to Ulithi on November 24.

After maintenance and training, she returned to Luzon on 14 December 14 with the fast-carrier task group. On December 17, *Alabama* had withdrawn to refuel but encountered Typhoon Cobra before doing so. By dawn the next day, weather conditions precluded refueling, with sustained winds of 50 knots and gusts to 83 knots, and the ship rolling up to 30 degrees. *Alabama*'s Kingfisher spotting planes were destroyed. *Alabama* made her way back to Ulithi, arriving on Christmas Eve. Soon thereafter, she steamed for Puget Sound for overhaul. Entering drydock there on January 18, *Alabama* remained in the shipyard until March 17, after which the ship and crew were subjected to standardization trials and refresher training off the California coast. She stood out for Pearl Harbor on April 4, arriving there on April 10. After a further week of training, she steamed for Ulithi, arriving April 28, 1945.

Leaving the anchorage on May 9, she steamed for the Ryukus to support the landings on Okinawa. On May 14, *Alabama*'s gunners brought down two Japanese aircraft.

Alabama again encountered a typhoon on June 3–4, suffering minor damage. Pressing on, *Alabama* shelled Minami Daito Shima on June 10.

On July 1, she steamed with the Third Fleet for the Japanese home islands. During the month, she shelled various industrial centers in Honshu, Hokkaido, Tokyo, and Kyushu.

On August 15, 1945, while off the southern coast of Hunshu, word was received that the Japanese had surrendered. Shortly thereafter, detachments of *Alabama*'s bluejackets and Marines went ashore for temporary duty as an occupying force. She entered Tokyo Bay on September 5 and, after taking men aboard, left Japanese waters on September 20, stopping at Okinawa to take aboard 700 homeward-bound men, primarily Seabees. *Alabama* entered San Francisco Bay on October 15. She hosted 9,000 visitors on Navy Day, October 27, before moving to San Pedro on October 29. On February 27, 1946, she stood out from San Pedro, steaming for the final time to Puget Sound for inactivation overhaul and layup.

On January 9, 1947, USS *Alabama* was decommissioned and placed in the reserve fleet.

Wearing Measure 12 (Modified) camouflage and displaying her number, "60," in white on her hull, aft of the anchor, USS *Alabama* steams off Norfolk Navy Yard on November 30, 1942. An SC air-search radar antenna is mounted on the top of the foremast. *National Archives*

Seen again on November 30, 1942, this time from off her starboard stern, *Alabama*'s number "60" is visible in white below the aircraft catapult. From this vantage point, the number 3 16-inch gun turret is nearly concealed from view by the catapult and the superstructure's aft end. *National Archives*

Seen here at rest in Casco Bay, Maine, during her shakedown cruise in December 1942, USS *Alabama* displays a Measure 12 (Modified) splotchy camouflage scheme consisting of Navy Blue (5-N) and Ocean Gray (5-O), with some areas of Haze Gray (5-H) also painted above the hull. There is a band of color on the hull, abeam of the mainmast, that seems to be lighter than the Ocean Gray paint applied on the hull. This band was possibly painted in Haze Gray. Two Vought OS2U Kingfisher floatplanes, used for observation and artillery spotting, are on the fantail. *Stan Piet collection*

Riding at anchor in Casco Bay in December 1942, *Alabama* is seen here from a more forward vantage point than in the previous photograph. No longer present on her superstructure deck are the two boat cranes that appeared in images of the ship taken during her commissioning. Removed at Norfolk, the cranes were already gone when *Alabama* began her shakedown cruise. *Naval History and Heritage Command*

Covers have been fitted over the canopies of the two Vought OS2U Kingfishers on *Alabama*'s port stern in this close-up view of the ship in Casco Bay. Details of the aircraft crane and portside catapult are visible. When the ship was riding at anchor, the US national flag was flown from the flagstaff on the fantail. *Naval History and Heritage Command*

As seagulls converge around *Alabama*'s stern, one of the ship's OS2U aircraft is poised above the aft starboard 40 mm gun mount. Visible in this image, probably taken at Casco Bay, is the boat boom that projects out from the top of the hull forward of the port catapult. Boats are moored to rope ladders that hang from the boom. *Stan Piet collection*

During a high-speed trial run of *Alabama* in the Atlantic in January 1943, the talker on the left is communicating on the telephone. Turrets 1 and 2 can be seen in the foreground, each of them featuring four ladders providing access to the roof over the gunhouse's frontal armor plate. The conning tower, distinguished by vision slits, and the navigating bridge are seen above turret 2. Atop the conning tower, in turn, are the forward Mk. 37 director and its Mk. 4 radar antenna for control of the 5-inch battery. Aft of the forward director are two other Mk. 37 directors. *Naval History and Heritage Command*

Seen here from *Alabama*'s bow during her shakedown cruise are two 20 mm antiaircraft guns on the starboard side of the main deck. Farther back, turrets 1 and 2 and also the twin 5-inch/38-caliber gun mounts are trained to starboard. Also trained to starboard is the Mk. 38 main-battery director atop the foretop. On the top of the Mk. 38 director, in turn, is a Mk. 8 fire-control radar that served to supplement the optical rangefinder that was built into the Mk. 38 director. *Naval History and Heritage Command*

The forward main-battery guns are here trained to starboard for firing practice during *Alabama*'s shakedown cruise near the northeast coast of the United States. In their designation as 16-inch/45-caliber Mk. 6 guns, the 45 caliber indicated that the length of the gun's bore was forty-five times the bore's diameter. On the side of the turret 1 gunhouse are two boxy objects. These objects are housings for the right trainer's telescope (*above*) and the pointer's telescope (*below and partly hidden*). *Naval History and Heritage Command*

All six of the 16-inch/45-caliber guns in turrets 1 and 2 fire a broadside to starboard sometime in late 1942 or early 1943. Depending on which ammunition she was firing, *Alabama* could fire as much as 48,600 pounds of projectiles per minute on a target as far away as 40,600 yards. *Naval History and Heritage Command*

Crewmen on the starboard side of turret 2 clean *Alabama*'s main deck of slush, following a storm during the ship's shakedown cruise. On the side of turret 1 is the rangefinder hood, which appears here as a large protrusion. The hood protected the 46-foot rangefinder's objective in the booth of the turret officer. *National Archives*

A turret 1 crewman wearing a watch cap and blue coveralls stands on a ladder on the turret's face to brush ice from a blast bag. "TURRET ONE" is inscribed in red on the back of the sailor's coveralls. Barrels were coated with grease for several feet to the front of the blast bags. *Naval History and Heritage Command*

Alabama trains her guns to starboard during battle practice in January 1943. In late 1942 and early 1943, USS *Alabama* went through an intense shakedown cruise. Due to the urgency of wartime, speed trials, crew familiarization, and practice for battle all had to be crammed into concentrated exercises. *Naval History and Heritage Command*

This forward-facing view of *Alabama*'s superstructure from the main deck's port side dates from January 1943. A quad 40 mm antiaircraft mount and the aft Mk. 38 director are to the right. About 50 feet higher than the aft Mk. 38 director was the forward Mk. 38 director, seen here at the top center of the image. *Naval History and Heritage Command*

Flying from the yardarm of *Alabama* in January 1943 are signal flags, seemingly antiquated communication tools that retained their usefulness as a means for ship-to-ship messaging while maintaining radio silence. A radio direction-finding (RDF) loop antenna is visible to the lower left. A quad 40 mm antiaircraft gun mount stands above the antenna. Near the top of this view is the forward Mk. 38 main-battery director, atop which is a Mk. 8 radar antenna. *Naval History and Heritage Command*

During a high-speed run on her shakedown cruise, *Alabama* vents boiler steam. In the background are turret 3 and the rear of the superstructure, while on the main deck to the left is a deck winch that was used for powering hawsers for docking and other operations. A gypsy head—as horizontally oriented capstans are called—is present on each side of the winch. The Mk. 8 radar antenna on the aft Mk. 38 director is here enveloped by a protective cover. *Naval History and Heritage Command*

Some features of the Measure 12 (Modified) camouflage scheme patterns on the 16-inch and 5-inch gunhouses, the Mk. 37 secondary-battery directors, and the superstructure are visible in this forward-looking view from aft of turret 3. In this January 1943 shot of *Alabama*, a gallery of three 20 mm antiaircraft gun mounts within a bulwark can be seen atop turret 3. Life rafts, stored two deep, are visible to the front of the bulwark. The 20 mm gun barrels are covered by canvas sleeve-type covers to protect them from the weather. *Naval History and Heritage Command*

Ready to launch, one of *Alabama*'s OS2U Kingfishers is poised on the starboard catapult in January 1943. Type P catapults, which were turntable mounted, launched aircraft by firing a powder charge. Also visible in this photograph are the (partly hidden) cage-like Mk. 8 radar antenna atop the Mk. 38 director above turret 3, a gallery of three 20 mm antiaircraft guns mounted on the top of turret 3 at the far right, two motor whaleboats sitting on dollies on the deck, and the extended boat boom to which rope ladders are attached on the starboard edge of the deck. *National Archives*

During a battle drill on USS *Alabama*'s shakedown cruise, this quad 40 mm antiaircraft gun mount crew is at general quarters. Their mount is located on the starboard side of the "house top"—the term used to designate the level atop the ship's navigating bridge. Visible inside a tub to the top left is the Mk. 51 director associated with this mount. Typically, Mk. 51 directors were positioned above and adjacent to the gun mount with which they were associated. This positioning afforded the Mk. 51 operators an all-around, unobstructed field of vision. *National Archives*

Bob Feller, sometimes known as "Bullet Bob," star pitcher for the Cleveland Indians professional baseball team, interrupted his career to enlist in the Navy. Feller went through gunnery school and, in the autumn of 1942, received his assignment to *Alabama*, aboard which he served as a gun captain for more than two years. During that period, Feller took part in a servicemen's all-star baseball game in which he struck out fifteen batters. *Naval Historical Foundation*

Flying above the Stars and Stripes on the fantail flagstaff of USS *Alabama* is the church pennant. The only flag or pennant authorized to fly over the US national ensign is the church pennant, which consists of a white field on which a dark-blue Latin cross is oriented on its side. This pennant is flown when church services are being conducted aboard the ship. The stern light staff, which is next to the flag staff, carries a white stern light over a blue stern light. Out of sight here is the wake light, yet another navigation light, which is located below the lower stern light. *Battleship USS Alabama Memorial Park*

Alabama returned from her shakedown cruise along the US Northeast to Chesapeake Bay on January 11, 1943. After undergoing one final week of shakedown exercises there, she reported to Norfolk Navy Yard for resupply and refitting. Here, and in several following images, we see *Alabama* as she appeared in the area of the Norfolk Navy Yard on February 7, 1943. Now repainted in Measure 22, Graded System camouflage, *Alabama* has been beefed up with two additional 20 mm antiaircraft guns and with bulwarks installed on the forecastle. *National Archives*

Atop turrets 2 and 3, quad 40 mm gun mounts have now replaced the earlier 20 mm guns, and the back of the air-defense level has been expanded. A gallery of three 20 mm antiaircraft guns is now installed behind a bulwark on both sides of the quarterdeck aft of turret 3. The wartime circles drawn on this photograph were intended to highlight modifications made in the course of the period that *Alabama* spent in the yard in early 1943. *National Archives*

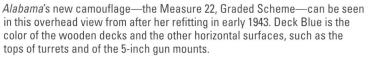

Alabama's new camouflage—the Measure 22, Graded Scheme—can be seen in this overhead view from after her refitting in early 1943. Deck Blue is the color of the wooden decks and the other horizontal surfaces, such as the tops of turrets and of the 5-inch gun mounts.

The holidays are coming, and a galley crewman checks out a turkey destined for a festive meal. Years later, a crewman remembered that everyone "paid for" such feasts by subsisting on lunch meat for days afterward. As was standard on most modern US warships, *Alabama* had a refrigeration plant so that meat and other perishables could be stored for some time. Cruises might be so long, however, that the stock of frozen food would run out, and the crew would thereafter have to manage on canned goods and dried foods. *Battleship USS Alabama Memorial Park*

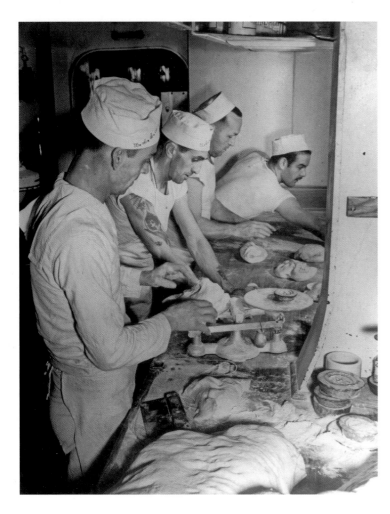

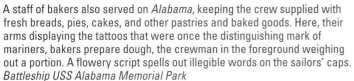

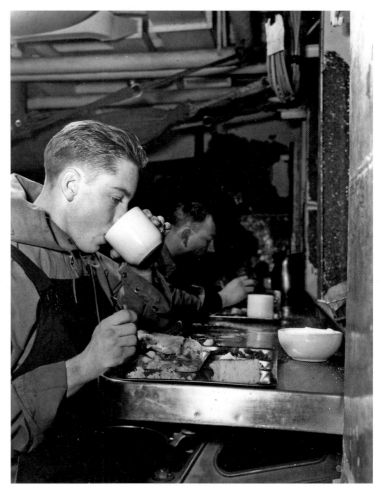

A staff of bakers also served on *Alabama*, keeping the crew supplied with fresh breads, pies, cakes, and other pastries and baked goods. Here, their arms displaying the tattoos that were once the distinguishing mark of mariners, bakers prepare dough, the crewman in the foreground weighing out a portion. A flowery script spells out illegible words on the sailors' caps. *Battleship USS Alabama Memorial Park*

It's mealtime aboard *Alabama*, sometime around January 1943. Food was more than adequate aboard the ship—some crewmen later remembered having gained a good deal of weight while serving aboard her. Holiday meals could be especially festive, but for long stretches, the fare was unremarkable. Beans were almost always a part of the meal—even some times at breakfast. Powdered eggs and creamed chipped beef on toast were other staples. *Battleship USS Alabama Memorial Park*

Cruising together during a joint deployment in the North Atlantic in 1943 are the sister ships USS *South Dakota* (*left*) and USS *Alabama*. The difference between the two vessels' camouflage is apparent: while *Alabama* wears Measure 22, Graded System, *South Dakota* is painted in Measure 21, with Navy Blue on vertical surfaces.

The Measure 22, Graded Scheme, applied to *Alabama* in February 1943 consisted of Navy Blue (5-N) from the black boot topping to the level of the lowest point of the main deck. Above the sheer, vertical surfaces were painted Haze Gray (5-H), and horizontal surfaces Deck Blue (20-B).

During 1943, *Alabama* spent time serving together with the British Home Fleet. Afterward, she returned to Norfolk Navy Yard for refitting. There, in August 1943, *Alabama*'s foremast was modified and a second SG radar antenna appeared on the top of her mainmast. To the superstructure atop the center twin 5-inch gun mount, two more Mk. 51 directors and tubs have been added on each side. Here, on August 20, 1943, *Alabama*—now painted in Measure 21 camouflage—departs Norfolk Navy Yard bound for service in the Pacific theater, where Measure 21 was preferred. *US Navy, A. D. Baker III collection*

Now painted in Measure 21's Navy Blue on all her above-waterline vertical surfaces and Deck Blue on her decks, *Alabama* is well prepared for service in the Pacific's blue waters as she sails past docks and out of the Norfolk Navy Yard on August 20, 1943. *US Navy, A. D. Baker III collection*

Two whaleboats can be seen stored on each side of the ventilator covers on *Alabama*'s quarterdeck in this August 20, 1943, view of the ship from above her stern following her refitting. While light-colored canvas covers protect some of the 20 mm antiaircraft guns, other 20 mm antiaircraft guns are enveloped in dark covers. *Naval History and Heritage Command*

Just a few moments in time separate from the previous photo is this August 20, 1943, aerial view of *Alabama*. Taken above the ship's bow at about noon that day, this image reveals the newly installed Mk. 40 director and its Mk. 3 radar antenna atop the conning tower. *Naval History and Heritage Command*

Assigned to Task Force 50, *Alabama* helped support US landings in the Gilbert Islands in the ship's first taste of combat in the Pacific in November and December 1943. Seen here on their way to the Gilberts are *Alabama*, light carrier USS *Monterey* (CVL-26), and, farther back, USS *Indiana* (BB-58). *Naval Historical Foundation*

On her way to the Pacific, *Alabama* crossed the equator—"the line" in maritime parlance—for the first time on September 2, 1943, necessitating a line-crossing Neptune party. By tradition, "pollywogs"—sailors who are making their first crossing of "the line"—must go through this initiation ceremony to become "shellbacks." The party shown here is believed to be from the first such observance held aboard *Alabama*. *Battleship USS Alabama Memorial Park*

Shellbacks wielding paddles form a gauntlet through which pollywogs must run during a line-crossing Neptune party aboard *Alabama*. Although it has been reported that the September 2, 1943, Neptune party inflicted no injuries upon the initiates, a few pollywogs managed to evade the ceremony. The side of turret 3's gunhouse is visible to the right. The starboard aircraft catapult can be seen in the center background, with a motor whaleboat to its right. *Battleship USS Alabama Memorial Park*

With *Alabama* resting in an anchorage, two teams of crewmen compete at tug-of-war on the ship's quarterdeck. Team sports built camaraderie, allowed crewmen to blow off steam, and improved morale and health. Although they worked long, hard hours, such recreational activity helped maintain the physical fitness that Navy men needed for battle readiness. One of the ship's Vought OS2U Kingfishers can be seen in the background, with the starboard catapult visible under its port wing. *Battleship USS Alabama Memorial Park*

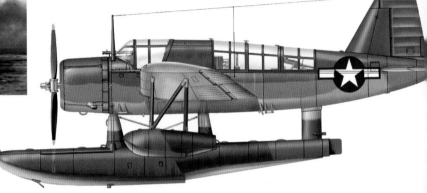

Throughout her operational career, USS *Alabama* had several Vought OS2U Kingfisher floatplanes assigned to her for observation and artillery-spotting duties. This Kingfisher assigned to the *Alabama* is depicted as it appeared in 1944. Typically, the Kingfisher had a range of 805 miles, a top speed of 164 m.p.h., and a ceiling of 13,000 feet.

Just weeks after supporting the US Marine landings on Tarawa and Betio in the Gilbert Islands, *Alabama* joined five other fast battleships on December 8, 1943, in bombarding Nauru Island, a source of phosphates for the Japanese military. Some of the effects of that bombardment, in which *Alabama* fired 535 shells, can be seen here. *Battleship USS Alabama Memorial Park*

In preparation for an invasion by the US Marine Corps, *Alabama* took part in a Fast Carrier Task Force raid on Japanese installations in the Marshall Islands in late January 1944. Seen here is the January 29–30 bombardment by *Alabama* of Roi-Namur island. In the course of the shelling, *Alabama* hurled 330 16-inch rounds and 1,562 5-inch rounds at enemy positions. *Battleship USS Alabama Memorial Park*

Following her service in the Marshall Islands operation and the mid-February 1944 bombardment of Truk, *Alabama* went on to the Marianas to unleash her massive firepower on Saipan, seen here, and on nearby Tinian. *Battleship USS Alabama Memorial Park*

Ever at the ready in case the signal for general quarters sounds, *Alabama* crewmen sleep with helmets and Mae West life vests close at hand. Sleeping quarters consist of racks, three bunks high, suspended from chains that sway in tandem with the rolling and pitching of the ship. Hammocks were also used by many crewmen, who found them comfortable after a period of adjustment. *Battleship USS Alabama Memorial Park*

Burial at sea was the norm for sailors who perished out on the ocean. Here, *Alabama*'s crew prepare to commit the bodies of several of their dead brethren to the deep. These men probably lost their lives in the so-called mount 5 incident, which took place on February 21, 1944. *Battleship USS Alabama Memorial Park*

Military honors are paid to deceased seamen whose bodies are being committed to the deep. Six body-bearers, dressed in whites, stand next to the body near the edge of the deck as attendees salute. During the burial service, if practicable, the ship would be stopped. *Battleship USS Alabama Memorial Park*

A ready service handling room was located directly underneath each of the dual-purpose 5-inch, 38-caliber mounts. Hoists for lifting shells and powder canisters connected the service handling room with the mount. In turn, the magazine and ammunition handling room, where powder and shells were separately stowed, was located below the service handling room. Ammunition hoists supplied powder and shells to the ready service handling room.

Chaplain George Markle visits a patient named Nolin—possibly Ernest H. Nolin—in *Alabama*'s sick bay on February 23, 1944—two days after the mount 5 incident. Nolin, who was not listed as having been wounded in the incident, appears well on his way to recovery. *Battleship USS Alabama Memorial Park*

Alabama suffered two particularly bad days on February 21–22, 1944, when the mount 5 incident was followed by Japanese air attacks on the ship and on Task Force 58, as it steamed off Saipan. This image, taken by someone aboard *Alabama* on February 22, shows a Japanese dive-bomber crashing into the ocean. *Naval History and Heritage Command*

Seen here from the forward tower aboard *Alabama*, a bright barrage of antiaircraft fire targets Japanese attackers during the raid on Saipan and Tinian. Tracers in the projectiles show up as streaks of light in the photograph, their squiggly appearance due to the camera's movement in the dim light. *Battleship USS Alabama Memorial Park*

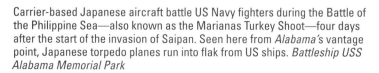

Carrier-based Japanese aircraft battle US Navy fighters during the Battle of the Philippine Sea—also known as the Marianas Turkey Shoot—four days after the start of the invasion of Saipan. Seen here from *Alabama's* vantage point, Japanese torpedo planes run into flak from US ships. *Battleship USS Alabama Memorial Park*

During the Battle of the Philippine Sea, a Japanese bomb that was dropped into the ocean explodes near *Alabama* on June 19, 1944. As stubborn and intense as the day's Japanese assault on Task Force 58 was, *Alabama* survived the battle unscathed. *Battleship USS Alabama Memorial Park*

Alabama crewmen line up for ice cream, a treat produced and distributed in impressive quantities by the ship. As on any US warship, *Alabama*'s gedunk—the counter where fountain drinks, candy bars, and snacks could be purchased— was one of the most popular spots on the vessel. *Battleship USS Alabama Memorial Park*

The *Alabama* wore an overall blue Measure 21 camouflage scheme during her initial operations in the Pacific in late 1943 and early 1944. During this period, the *Alabama* also began to receive upgraded radars and an increasing number of antiaircraft weapons. The Navy Blue hull and superstructure, combined with the Deck Blue decks, allowed the battleship to blend into the sea when viewed from the air, but did tend to silhouette the ship against the horizon when viewed from the surface.

Alabama underwent refitting at the Puget Sound Navy Yard in early 1945. Inclining experiments were being conducted on the vessel toward the end of the refitting when this picture was taken on February 20, 1945. The purpose of the tests was to determine how stable the ship was, where its center of gravity lay, and to set its lightship weight—the ship's weight minus cargo, ammunition, crew, water, and fuel. One of the most apparent modifications that resulted from the refitting was the repainting of *Alabama* in Measure 22, Graded System camouflage. *National Archives*

Another modification made during *Alabama*'s overhaul in early 1945 was the addition of new radar installations and antennas. This aft-facing view of the front of the forward tower shows the dish-type SK-2 radar antenna now fitted near the top of the foremast. At 17 feet in diameter, the SK-2 air-search radar antenna was a replacement for the SC radar that had formerly been positioned on the top of the foremast. One of the TDY electronic-countermeasures (ECM) jammers was contained in the radome that is positioned over the top of the SK-2 antenna. *NARA San Bruno via usnavyresearch.com*

Seen here from *Alabama*'s starboard side are the redesigned foremast with the newly installed radar and ECM devices as they appeared at Puget Sound Navy Yard on March 13, 1945. The SK-2 radar was able to track aircraft up to 100 nautical miles away and as high as 10,000 feet. The TDY ECM device visible above the radar could jam enemy radio transmissions. In addition, there were other ECM antennas mounted on or below the air defense level on the forward yardarm, and still more on the superstructure's first level. *NARA San Bruno via usnavyresearch.com*

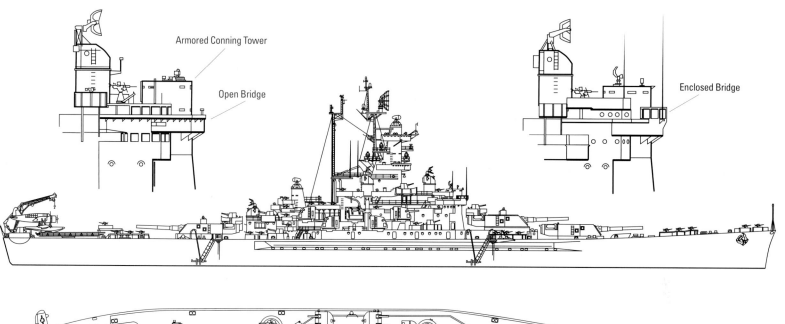

Armored Conning Tower

Open Bridge

Enclosed Bridge

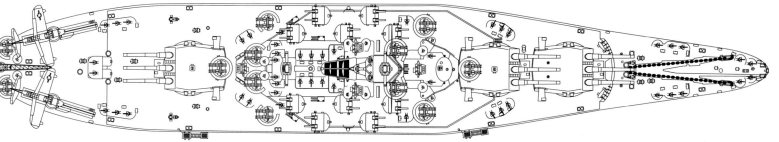

For most of her service life, *Alabama* had an open navigating bridge, as shown at left. However, during her February 1945 yard period at Puget Sound the navigating bridge was enclosed, as shown at right. By March 1945, as depicted here, the decks of *Alabama* were cluttered with an array of 20mm and 40mm antiaircraft weapons, a marked change from the relatively clean lines she displayed when commissioned. To man these weapons, not only was more electronics gear needed, but so were more men, and *Alabama's* complement increased from 1,849 to about 2,350.

This view and the next three photos reflect the appearance of *Alabama* during a trial run in Puget Sound just after her refitting. The ship's newly applied Measure 22, Graded System camouflage is here on display on March 12, 1945. *US Navy, A. D. Baker III collection*

Motor whaleboats stowed on the quarterdeck flank the sides of the ventilator covers, above which is the tub for the two 20 mm guns located aft of turret 3. In this March 12, 1945, view of *Alabama* from off her port stern, a pile of supplies are visible on the deck between the catapults. *US Navy, A. D. Baker III collection*

The updated foremast and mainmast and their new radar and ECM devices are readily apparent in this aerial view from off the port side of USS *Alabama* on March 15, 1945. Here the mainmast, which was previously much shorter than the foremast, is now greatly extended. *US Navy, A. D. Baker III collection*

The date is March 22, 1945, and *Alabama* is once more at sea. She sailed for San Diego for a short training period following her overhaul at Bermerton. *Alabama*'s aircraft are now Curtiss SC-1 Seahawks, which have replaced the OS2Us. Two Seahawks are on the ship's two catapults, and a third can be seen between them. *US Navy, A. D. Baker III collection*

The *Alabama* was repainted in the blue and gray Measure 22 camouflage scheme for her later operations in the Pacific. This scheme was also worn during the *Alabama's* operations in the Atlantic in 1943. The Navy Blue hull blended into the sea, while the Haze Gray paint on the superstructure made that part of the vessel less obvious on the horizon. The *Alabama* also received newer radar equipment and additional antiaircraft weapons to deal with the ever-increasing threat of Japanese kamikaze attacks.

Late in April 1945, *Alabama* returned to the ranks of Task Force 58 to support the invasion of Okinawa. Task Group 58.3 was carrying out a carrier raid on Kyushu airfields on May 14 when a photographer aboard *Alabama* captured this image of a kamikaze blasting into USS *Enterprise* (CV-6). *Battleship USS Alabama Memorial Park*

Combat is intensifying and there is now more flak in the skies over Task Group 58.3 on May 14, 1945. The crews of two 20 mm antiaircraft guns on *Alabama*'s starboard side quarterdeck are prepared to open fire as, in the distance, left of the center of the view, a Japanese plane hits the water and explodes. *Battleship USS Alabama Memorial Park*

Going down in flames over a Curtiss Seahawk on *Alabama*'s starboard catapult, the Japanese aircraft seen in the preceding photo is the fifth and last one to target Task Group 58.3 on May 14, 1945. To the lower left of the image, a 20 mm gun continues to fire at the falling Japanese plane. *Naval History and Heritage Command*

The warship in the foreground is engaged in an underway replenishment operation (UNREP) with *Alabama* in the background. To carry out an UNREP operation, two ships would have to maintain close formation at a stable distance from each other. Crewmen on the two ships would rig high lines along which supplies and fuel would be transferred from one vessel to the other. In this image, crewmen in the foreground handle supply-laden canvas panniers marked "USS ALABAMA 10 DIV," referring to the 10th Division of the ship, which comprised a portion of the 20 mm and 40 mm antiaircraft batteries. *Battleship USS Alabama Memorial Park*

Alabama crewmen are the congregation at divine services being conducted on the ship's fantail. Shade has been provided by a cover rigged over the area, and the altar and the chaplain can be made out in the background in the shadows. One wing of each of the Seahawk aircraft has been folded. *Battleship USS Alabama Memorial Park*

Docked side by side at the foot of Telegraph Hill in late October 1945 are the three sister ships (*left to right*): *Indiana*, *Massachusetts*, and *Alabama*. Eager to take a close look at these distinguished veterans, thousands of visitors flocked to the battleships on Navy Day, October 27. *Battleship USS Alabama Memorial Park*

Still wearing the Measure 22, Graded System camouflage she received in early 1945, *Alabama* steams off an arid coast. Sailors dressed in whites can be seen assembled in different places on the deck, suggesting that the battleship was either about to make port or was just leaving one. In this photo, likely from the period after the end of World War II, the ship's three Curtiss SC-1 Seahawks can still be seen on the catapults and in the fantail. *US Naval Institute*

In honor of the John Paul Jones bicentennial on July 6, 1947, *Alabama* opened her decks to the public while laid up at Pier 91 in the reserve fleet at Puget Sound, Washington. Sea Scouts assisted the naval personnel working on the ship and also the crew of the carrier *Ticonderoga*, which was also open to the public that day. Here the gun mount atop the turret is visible, though most of the 40 mm mounts are enveloped in cocoons. All the radar antennas on *Alabama* are still in place. In keeping with a plan to reconfigure *Alabama* for helicopters, both of the battleship's catapults were removed sometime between February 1949 and September 1952. In the event, however, *Alabama* was never fitted for helicopters.

CHAPTER 3
Memorial

When the Second World War ended, the United States commanded the most massive naval armada ever created. A nation at peace had no need of such an enormous force, however, and efforts began almost immediately to cut back the fleet by some 75 percent. Older vessels and those with war damage were scrapped or used for target practice.

At their maximum, the officers and men aboard *Alabama* numbered 2,500.

As with all ships in the Navy, turnover and reassignment of crewmen took place. Eventually a total of 6,322 men were to serve proudly aboard *Alabama*, a vessel that gained the reputation of being lucky. Although she took part in some of the best-known engagements of World War II and endured two typhoons, *Alabama* lost a grand total of only five men in the theater of combat, none of them due to enemy action. Through all the adversities, *Alabama* sheltered her crew, providing them security while they slept, ate, watched movies, played sports, and, naturally, worked and fought against would-be world-conquering enemies.

Alabama was one of the Navy's newest battleships, and it had come through the war almost without a scratch. Instead of scrapping *Alabama*, it was decided that she should join the Reserve Fleet. Ships in the Reserve Fleet, which is often called the Mothball Fleet, are reserved, available to be rapidly recalled should a national emergency arise. *Alabama* was laid up in Bremerton, Washington, where the crew set about removing all the ship's ammunition and perishable items. An inventory was conducted of each of the ship's compartments. Preservative coatings were applied to all exposed metal. Items on the ship's exterior that were prone to rapid deterioration in the weather were removed and stowed belowdecks. A coat of antifouling compound was applied to the hull, and the ship's interior was sealed. All the vessel's hatches, the funnel, gun muzzles, and director ports were sealed. Dehumidification equipment ensured that the battleship's interior would be maintained at 25 to 30 percent humidity. Metal cocoons were installed around the ship's

40 mm quad mounts, and desiccant materials were placed inside the weapons for preservation. In order to preserve *Alabama*'s underwater structure, the ship was drydocked and the hull was recoated every five years, initially. By 1957, however, this practice gave way to the method of cathodic protection, which prevents rust buildup by applying an electric current to the hull. The current acts on anodes that are suspended near the ship under the water.

Alabama was officially stricken from the Navy list on June 1, 1962, having been active only for five years and having accrued only 218,000 miles at sea. The four sisters—*Alabama*, *South Dakota*, *Indiana*, and *Massachusetts*—were declared obsolete and Navy surplus. Nevertheless, the ships' fates were not identical. Like *Alabama*, *Indiana* had been laid up in Bremerton, but while *Indiana* was towed out for the ship breakers on October 24, 1963, *Alabama* remained. Mothballed on the East Coast, *South Dakota* suffered a fate similar to that of *Indiana*. *Alabama*, however, was spared, thanks to the efforts of citizens of the state of Alabama, who raised the funds needed to tow the battleship to Mobile from Bremerton—a total of 5,600 miles. Money was also collected to provide for a park and for refurbishing the ship to serve as a memorial to US veterans.

A channel—2 miles long, 120 feet wide, and 32 feet deep—was dug in the bottom of Mobile Bay to allow the massive *Alabama*—with its 22-foot draft and 108-foot beam—an anchorage. A total of 2.7 million cubic yards of earth were dug up to create the channel, and this material served as landfill to create the park in the adjacent area. More than thirteen million people have visited *Alabama* since she was opened to the public on January 9, 1965. The battleship was also used as the set for *Under Siege*, a 1992 Hollywood action-thriller starring Steven Seagal and Tommy Lee Jones. Over the years, two hurricanes have struck the ship, which suffered only minimal damage, while providing her staff with shelter, just as she had afforded shelter to her crews during Pacific typhoons in her youth.

A PROPOSED PROJECTION OF

BATTLESHIP U.S.S. ALABAMA MEMORIAL PARK

DEWEY CROWDER ASSOCIATES, AIA
ARCHITECT – ENGINEER – PLANNER

FOR

U.S.S. ALABAMA BATTLESHIP COMMISSION

After the US Navy announced plans to scrap the battleship USS *Alabama* (BB-60) in 1962, the USS *Alabama* Memorial Commission was established, to preserve the battleship as a museum ship and memorial to Alabamians who served in the military in World War II and the Korean War. Dewey Crowder Associates submitted this proposed design for the Battleship USS *Alabama* Memorial Park in Mobile, which, along with the moored ship, would have included several pavilions and buildings, gardens, displays of aircraft and vehicles, and monuments.

After only four years and five months of active service, USS *Alabama* had been decommissioned on January 9, 1947, and, as part of the Pacific Reserve Fleet, had been placed in long-term storage at Bremerton, Washington. Following a successful fundraising campaign by the USS *Alabama* Memorial Commission, the US Navy authorized the transfer of the ship to the state of Alabama on June 16, 1964. On that date, on a dock at the Puget Sound Naval Shipyard, Bremerton, alongside *Alabama*, Capt. James G. Thwing, USNR (Ret.), *right*, who would become the first director of the USS *Alabama* Battleship Memorial Park, and Cmdr. J. G. Gillespie, commanding officer of the Bremerton Reserve Group, are signing documents transferring the battleship to the state of Alabama.

When *Alabama* departed from Bremerton for Mobile, Alabama, in June 1964, the tubs for the 40 mm gun mounts still had shelter domes over them. Spot priming is evident on the turrets and other structures. Most of the rigging and radar and communications antennas had been removed when the ship went into long-term storage. The USS *Alabama* Memorial Commission budgeted $25,000 to prepare the battleship for going to sea.

In 1964, the goal of the USS *Alabama* Memorial Commission was to raise one million dollars to bring the battleship to Mobile Bay and establish the memorial park. By spring 1964, the commission had succeeded in collecting $800,000. Signs like this one, photographed around March 1964, were part of the fundraising drive. To the front are GSgt. Alley Pensey, USMC; CPO William Rhodes, USN; and 1Sgt. Paul Lamneck, USMC.

Stripped of much of its equipment for long-term storage, *Alabama* rides high in the water at Bremerton not long before beginning its journey to Mobile. Work to prepare the ship for the long voyage under tow consumed thirty days. The 5-inch/38-caliber dual-purpose guns and the directors for the main and secondary batteries were left in place during the period of storage.

On June 16, 1964, a photographer on a Puget Sound ferry boat snapped this view of *Alabama* being towed into the sound on the occasion of the battleship's departure for Seattle, the first stop on the long voyage to Mobile. The battleship would be towed the entire distance, via the Panama Canal. Of the $1 million budget for establishing the USS *Alabama* Memorial Park, $300,000 was set aside for towing and insurance charges from Puget Sound to Mobile Bay.

Tugboats are towing *Alabama* past a point of land on Puget Sound around June 18, 1964. The dome shelters were still on the tubs of all of the 40 mm gun mounts. A temporary shelter is on the deck aft of turret number 3.

During a workup at the Todd Shipyard at Seattle, *Alabama* was made seaworthy, and towing gear for the sea voyage was installed on the battleship. When the ship departed from Seattle, only the dome shelters on the fantail gun tubs were still present. The ship is shown here being towed away from the dock. The ship departed from the port on July 21, 1964.

With the Space Needle dominating the Seattle skyline, *Alabama* has been towed from her berth, and harbor tugboats that had assisted her are departing. From here, *Alabama* would be towed by oceangoing tugs *Sea Lion* and *Sea Ranger.* In a tragic mishap, *Sea Lion* would sink off the coast of Panama on August 22, 1964, while towing *Alabama*, resulting in the drowning of one crewman. The rest of the crew were saved.

Battleship *Alabama* is being towed into Balboa Harbor, Panama, at the beginning of her transit of the Panama Canal. Four tugs are visible: one to the front, two on the battleship's port beam, and one aft. To the left is the Bridge of the Americas, which had been completed two years before.

Assisted by towing locomotives, *Alabama* has just cleared the Miraflores Locks of the Panama Canal in late July 1964. Tugboats are approaching to resume towing the battleship along the canal.

A series of towing locomotives on each side of *Alabama* are pulling her along one of the locks of the Panama Canal.

In a photo taken from directly above *Alabama* as it transits a lock of the Panama Canal, the tight clearance is obvious, with only approximately 1 foot between each side of the hull and the inner walls of the lock. A very dark paint or stain existed on the wooden parts of the main deck and the 01 level.

After a nearly two-month transit from Seattle, *Alabama* arrived at her destination in Mobile Bay on September 14, 1964. She is shown here under tow in the bay. The starboard anchor chain, which was draped along the side of the foredeck, casts a squiggly shadow on the side of the hull.

The poor condition of the hull and forward turrets of *Alabama* upon arrival in Mobile Bay is evident in this photo taken from the port beam. Before departing Bremerton, the ship's propellers were removed. One of the propellers is visible on the foredeck, slightly aft of the ship's number, "60."

Turret 3 and the rear of the superstructure and adjacent gun mounts are the focus of a view taken shortly after *Alabama*'s arrival in Mobile Bay. Air-search, surface-search, and antiaircraft radar antennas had been restored to their positions on the ship, including on the aft Mk. 37 gun director at the upper center of this photo, during the ship's recent time in Seattle.

At her new berth on Mobile Bay, work on refurbishing *Alabama* for display commenced on October 7, 1964. As seen from aft of turret number 3, a crane is removing a propeller from the ship. The propeller would be displayed in the memorial park near the ship. During the refurbishment, the entire exterior of the ship was cleaned and painted, as well as the initial interior spaces that would be open to the public.

Members of a Marine honor guard are presenting arms during the ceremony opening battleship *Alabama* to the public on January 9, 1965. Working in two ten-hour shifts of eight men each, work crews had succeeded in restoring the ship to admirable condition in just three months.

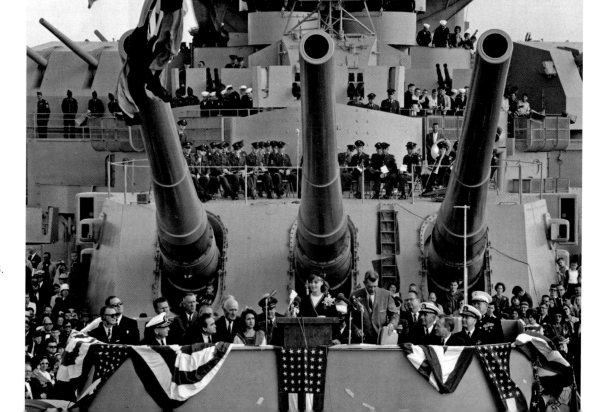

Dignitaries are gathered inside a splinter shield to the rear of turret 3 during the dedication ceremony of the USS *Alabama* Memorial Park, on January 9, 1965. Undersecretary of the Navy Paul B. Fay Jr., *to the right of the podium*, officially transferred the battleship to Gov. George C. Wallace, *seated to the left of the podium*, representing the citizens of Alabama. An Army band is seated on the roof of turret 3.

One of two surviving South Dakota–class battleships (*Massachusetts* [BB-59] is preserved at Fall River, Massachusetts), *Alabama* is maintained in an excellent state of preservation at Mobile, Alabama. The ship is viewed from the forecastle, with the breech of a 20 mm antiaircraft gun in the left foreground. The guns, spanning from 16-inch/45-caliber down to 20 mm, present an impressive display.

An overall view of the starboard side of *Alabama* around 2007 demonstrates the battleship's location with respect to the memorial park on the opposite side of the ship. Before the ship was brought to rest at this location in 1964, the USS *Alabama* Memorial Commission budgeted half a million dollars for dredging her berthing area and constructing the 75-acre memorial park.

Alabama is observed off her starboard bow, the curve of the top of the hull casting a large shadow on the bow. The long, recessed area on the hull below the main deck amidships represents the top of the shell blister, which formed a sloped catwalk with access ports for fueling.

The ship is viewed from closer to her bow. Surrounding the ship is a watertight cofferdam, constructed in the first few years of the twenty-first century. This enabled water to be pumped out so periodic repairs and maintenance could be made to the hull without moving the ship to drydock.

A close-up of the port bow shows the port anchor, the ship's number, and draft marks: white numbers that indicate how the ship was riding with reference to its waterline. On the forecastle are two 20 mm guns with shields, positioned inside splinter shields, also called gun tubs or bulwarks.

The port amidships area of *Alabama* is viewed from the ground, spanning from turret number 1 aft to almost the rear of the superstructure. The large, dish-shaped antenna on the foremast is for the SK-2 air-search radar. Below and forward of the SK-2 radar is the forward Mk. 38 main-battery director; the aft Mk. 38 director is to the right of the photo, atop the tapered aft fire-control tower. Both Mk. 38 directors have Mk. 8 fire-control radar antennas on top of them.

As seen from off the port stern, the aircraft crane towers above the fantail. The crane was used to lift the battleship's scout planes from the surface of the ocean, back up to the two catapults. The top of the starboard catapult is visible above the fantail.

Flanking the aircraft crane are two quadruple 40 mm gun mounts, located in splinter shields with sponsons below them. Aft of the crane is the ensign staff. The port catapult is not mounted, but the upper part of the starboard catapult is visible above the hull.

In a view of the aft part of *Alabama* from the port side, just forward of the aft 40 mm gun mounts and aircraft crane are two raised tubs; these contained Mk. 51 directors for the 40 mm guns. Just aft of the raised guns of turret 3 is a gallery of three 20 mm guns on the quarterdeck. A similar gallery is on the opposite side of the deck. Above them is a raised platform and bulwark for two 20 mm antiaircraft guns, a feature added in early 1945. Below the hook on the end of the aircraft crane is the kingpost for the port boat boom. This kingpost supported the boom, visible along the top of the hull immediately aft of the kingpost.

A quadruple 40 mm gun mount and its circular bulwark on the fantail are viewed from the piece's right side. The seat in the foreground was occupied by the trainer, who, when the gun was under local control (that is, not being controlled by a nearby director), controlled the azimuth of the guns. The dark-colored devices on top of the guns' receivers are autoloaders, into which crewmen fed clips of ammunition. The curved objects on the rears of the receivers are spent-casing deflectors.

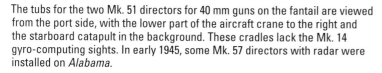

The tubs for the two Mk. 51 directors for 40 mm guns on the fantail are viewed from the port side, with the lower part of the aircraft crane to the right and the starboard catapult in the background. These cradles lack the Mk. 14 gyro-computing sights. In early 1945, some Mk. 57 directors with radar were installed on *Alabama.*

A Mk. 51 Mod. 2 director is displayed with the Mk. 14 gyro-computing sight installed. The view is from the operator's perspective, with box-shaped counterweights on the upper outboard sides of the unit, the light-gray sight at the upper center, and the operator's handlebars at the bottom. The operator of the Mk. 51 director used the handlebars to slew and elevate the sight. Once he acquired and tracked a target, the sight computed a firing solution and transmitted that information to the 40 mm gun mount, whose powered elevating and traversing mechanisms brought the guns onto the target. Except when the gun crew exercised local control (that is, when they took over the training, pointing, and firing of the guns), the director controlled those functions.

The ensign flies from its staff on the aft end of the fantail of *Alabama*.

The aircraft crane could be traversed 360 degrees. In addition to handling scout planes, it was used for lifting and lowering the ship's boats and supplies.

The upper part of the aircraft crane is shown, with the cradle for the director for the starboard fantail 40 mm gun mount to the right and the masts in the background. The vertical pole to the left is for supporting a cable with lights attached, the forward end of which is attached to the foremast.

The aircraft catapult in the starboard position is viewed from its left side. The catapult is mounted on the large, drum-shaped pedestal. On the edge of the deck to the front of the catapult is the kingpost for the starboard boat boom. When the ship was underway, the kingpost would be swung down forward and stored against the top of the hull.

The starboard aircraft catapult, seen here from the forward end, is not original to *Alabama* and was salvaged from a cruiser. On the top of each side of the catapult are shock absorbers, which cushioned and stopped the launching car, on which the center float of the scout plane rested. The launching car was propelled by a powder charge. Catwalks are on each side of the catapult.

The catapult is seen from its left rear, with turret 3 and the starboard side of its superstructure in the background. Initially, Vought OS2U Kingfishers were the scout planes embarked on *Alabama*. They were replaced in March 1945 by Curtiss SC-1 Seahawks.

A gallery of three 20 mm antiaircraft guns are located on each side of the quarterdeck aft of turret 3; the starboard one is shown. Each gun mount has an armored shield with two panels, and all three guns have additional protection in the splinter shield, or bulwark, to their front. Ammunition magazines are mounted on these guns.

Facing forward from the fantail, a platform and splinter shield for two 20 mm antiaircraft guns are perched above several large ventilator hoods. Grouped near these ventilators are a hatch to belowdecks, hose reels, equipment lockers, and a capstan. Farther forward is turret number 3 and the rear of the superstructure.

A view from an upper level of the rear of the superstructure, facing aft, shows the aircraft catapult (*left*), the aircraft crane flanked by quadruple 40 mm gun mounts and their directors, two 20 mm gun mounts atop ventilators (below the 16-inch gun barrels), and the Mk. 12 radar antenna of the aft Mk. 37 secondary-battery director (*right*).

In a view from the starboard side of the aft part of the superstructure, looming in the foreground, atop the aft fire-control tower, is the aft Mk. 38 main-battery director, with a Mk. 8 fire-control radar antenna mounted over it. This director and the forward main-battery director contained crewmen and equipment for acquiring and tracking targets for the 16-inch guns.

A photo of most of the port side of the superstructure and the amidships part of the hull shows the recess in the upper part of the hull formed by the top of the shell blister and, above it, the overhang of the main deck. The relative positions of the quadruple 40 mm and the twin 5-inch/38-caliber gun mounts alongside the superstructure, the aft primary and secondary battery directors, and, *far right*, the 20 mm gun gallery and splinter shield atop turret 3 are shown.

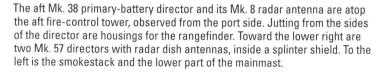

The aft Mk. 38 primary-battery director and its Mk. 8 radar antenna are atop the aft fire-control tower, observed from the port side. Jutting from the sides of the director are housings for the rangefinder. Toward the lower right are two Mk. 57 directors with radar dish antennas, inside a splinter shield. To the left is the smokestack and the lower part of the mainmast.

The upper part of the mainmast, including the yardarm, the teardrop-shaped work platform, the rectangular SR air-search radar antenna, and, atop the mast, the SG surface-search radar antenna. The view was taken from the front of the mainmast.

This quadruple 40 mm gun mount is sited within a semicircular splinter shield alongside the starboard side of the superstructure. Conical flash suppressors are on the muzzles of the guns. A ring sight is visible through the vision slot on the near side of the gun shield. Above this mount is a quadruple 40 mm gun mount on the aft part of the superstructure.

The quadruple 40 mm gun mount on the main deck abeam the port side of the aft part of the superstructure is viewed from its right side, with the aircraft crane visible in the background. The trainer's tractor-type seat is below the side of the armored shield. Another quad 40 mm gun mount is to the left, on level 01.

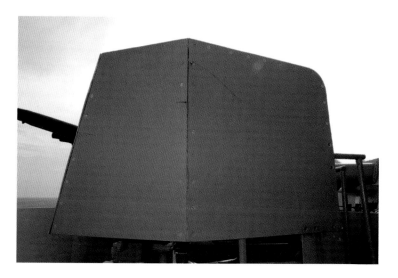

Two armor plates constitute the left side of the shield of the quadruple 40 mm gun mount. The plates are attached to a frame with slotted, flathead screws.

Behind the left side of the armored shield of the quadruple 40 mm gun mount is the pointer's station, with a ring-and-bead sight, below which is the black-painted elevating handwheel and the elevating worm-gear case. Below the tube that supports the ring-and-bead sight is the elevation indicator.

A view forward from the center of the quadruple 40 mm gun mount shows the inboard 40 mm guns, their cradles, and the center armored plate of the shield. On the sides of the receivers are the hand-operating levers. Atop the receivers are ammunition autoloaders. Below the receivers are elevating sectors.

The trainer's station, on the right side of the quad 40 mm gun mount, includes a ring-and-bead sight, below which are the train correspondence indicator, the manual training handwheel, the trainer's seat, and his foot rests.

The ring-and-bead sight for the trainer of a quadruple 40 mm gun mount is visible through the slot in the shield. In a tub on the superstructure above the ring sight is a Mk. 57 director, with a Mk. 12 radar antenna on the front. In the left background are two 20 mm antiaircraft guns with Mk. 14 gyro gunsights installed.

A pedestal and cradle for a Mk. 51 director is seen from the rear inside its splinter shield. This cradle would have held a Mk. 14 gyro gunsight, as also seen on the 20 mm guns toward the lower left of the preceding photo. Radar-equipped Mk. 57 directors began to supplant the Mk. 51s on *Alabama* in early 1945. The operator maneuvered the director with two handlebars. To the upper left of the cradle is a bar for mounting a ring sight on the front; a bead sight remains on the rear of the bar.

The cradle for a Mk. 51 director is protruding above its splinter shield, on the main deck. This director was associated with a quadruple 40 mm gun mount on the main deck abeam the starboard side of the aft part of the superstructure. To the left is the right-hand carriage.

In the foreground is a Mk. 57 director in an armored tub, with the Mk. 38 primary-battery director and Mk. 8 radar antenna forming the backdrop. The Mk. 57 director employed a radar set with a dish antenna to provide the 40 mm antiaircraft guns with a blind-firing capability. *Alabama* first acquired these directors in early 1945.

A quadruple 40 mm gun mount on *Alabama* is observed from the rear, inside a splinter shield. The barrels of the 40 mm guns were water-cooled, and two tanks for coolant water are on the rear of the platform of the gun mount, below guardrails. Curved, black spent-casing deflectors are on the rears of the gun receivers. Manuals for these gun mounts refer to the vertical strips and corner pieces to which the armored plates are screwed as butt straps.

Two Mk. 57 directors on the rear part of the superstructure are in the foreground, with the aft Mk. 8 fire-control radar and the mainmast above them. The large antenna on the mainmast is for the SR air-search radar.

On the superstructure forward of the single smokestack is the forward fire-control tower, which includes the air-defense platform at the top, above which is the forward Mk. 38 primary-battery director.

Both of the Mk. 38 primary-battery directors are visible in this photo taken from the port-aft quarter of *Alabama*'s superstructure. The forward Mk. 38 is toward the top, and the aft one is to the right of center. Also in view are the port and the aft Mk. 37 directors: respectively, left of center, and lower right. A Mk. 57 director, with dish radar antenna, is in a tub toward the right.

The forward fire-control tower is seen from the lower-aft quarter, at the top of which are the antiaircraft-spotting platform and the forward Mk. 38 director and Mk. 8 fire-control radar antenna. On the foremast, mounted on the tower, is the SK-2 air-search radar antenna. The pod aft of the SK-2 antenna contains the DBM radar direction-finder antenna.

Two searchlight platforms are on the rear of the fire-control tower; the upper one has two 36-inch searchlights, and the lower one a 24-inch unit. The open bridge toward the bottom of the tower is part of the secondary conning station. Jutting from the top front and sides of this bridge and of the forward air-defense station at the top of the tower were wind deflectors, called windshields. A steam whistle is below the secondary-conning bridge.

The Mk. 37 director on the port side of the superstructure, designated secondary-battery director number 2, is viewed from above, facing aft. The director is facing outward; jutting from the side is a sheet-metal cover that was placed over the right side of the rangefinder when the battleship was placed in long-term storage after World War II. Mounted above the director is a combination of two radar antennas: the larger one is for the Mk. 12 fire-control radar, and the smaller, curved one on the near side of the Mk. 12 is for the Mk. 22 height-finder radar.

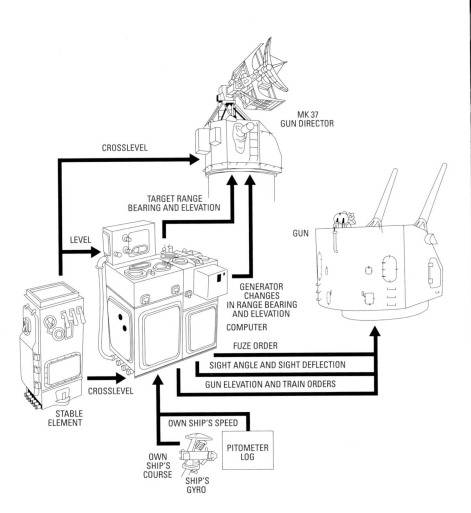

CROSSLEVEL

MK 37
GUN DIRECTOR

TARGET RANGE
BEARING AND ELEVATION

LEVEL

GUN

GENERATOR
CHANGES
IN RANGE BEARING
AND ELEVATION

COMPUTER

FUZE ORDER

SIGHT ANGLE AND SIGHT DEFLECTION

GUN ELEVATION AND TRAIN ORDERS

CROSSLEVEL

STABLE
ELEMENT

OWN SHIP'S SPEED

OWN
SHIP'S
COURSE

PITOMETER
LOG

SHIP'S
GYRO

The Mk. 37 secondary battery director usually was tasked with tracking enemy aircraft and ships, primarily destroyers, and establishing their range, bearing, and, in the case of aircraft, altitude. Those data were transmitted to the plotting room ("Plot"), where analog computers, working with stable elements, which corrected for the pitch and roll of the ship, and the ship's gyro and pitometer, which provided information on the ship's course and speed, calculated within seconds the firing solution for the 5-inch guns. Plot sent that data to the director as well as the 5-inch turret and also controlled the train (traverse) and elevation of both the guns and the director. However, the director also made corrections to the target bearing, range, and angle of attack. Also, although the directors normally controlled the aiming and firing of the 5-inch guns, Plot or the gun crews could control the guns when necessary. Plot would control the guns when firing at targets ashore.

Operators in the cramped confines of the director tracked targets by using the unit's optical rangefinder and fire-control radar, transmitting that information to fire-control computers, which then sent firing solutions to the ship's 5-inch/38-caliber gun mounts.

A rear view of the Mk. 37 director shows the Mk. 12 with Mk. 22 antenna combination. The latter antenna's resemblance to a segment of orange peel gave rise to its nickname of "orange-peel antenna."

In a view facing aft from the port side of the secondary conning bridge on the forward fire-control tower, in the left foreground is the front of the top of the smokestack, with handrails and rungs on it and a catwalk around it. At the center are two whip antennas. To the lower right are twin 5-inch/38-caliber gun mount number 10 and Mk. 37 secondary director number 2.

In a wider-perspective view taken from the same place as the preceding photo, the lower part of the mainmast is to the rear of the smokestack, with a ladder on the starboard side of it.

The entire top front of the smokestack is displayed, including a view of its starboard side and three of the whip antennas and their bases. The catwalk around it constitutes a grille, with a steel frame with steel bars. To the lower left is twin 5-inch/38-caliber gun mount number 7.

The port side of the top of the smokestack is seen from the aft end of the port side of the secondary conning station on the forward fire-control station. In the foreground is a ladder.

Twin 5-inch/38-caliber dual-purpose gun mount number 9, the aft mount of this type on the starboard side, is viewed from the upper rear. These installations are referred to as mounts, never turrets. The entire enclosure, including the roof, is called the shield or the gunhouse. On the rear of the roof is the mount captain's hatch, locked in the closed position with a dog on each side that was operated from inside the mount.

Adjacent to twin 5-inch/38-caliber gun mount number 10, on the port side of the second superstructure deck, also called the 02 level, are two 5-inch loading machines, seen here from the rear. These were practice devices that allowed members of the gun crews to perform loading drills without doing so in the confines of the actual gun mount. Between the loading machines are two practice projectile hoists.

The 5-inch loading machines and practice projectile hoists are viewed from the front, with twin 5-inch/38-caliber gun mount number 10 to the right.

Seen from the port side of the forward superstructure are twin 5-inch gun mounts numbers 2 (*upper*) and 4. When gun mounts were on both sides of the longitudinal centerline of a US Navy ship, those of a given type on the starboard side were assigned odd numbers, from forward to aft, and those on the port side had even numbers. The pod with the dome top to the far right is for a TDY electronic-countermeasures jammer.

The port side of *Alabama* from turret number 1 to the rear of the superstructure is depicted, with details of the forward fire-control tower, the quadruple 40 mm and twin 5-inch/38-caliber gun mounts, and the primary- and secondary-battery directors.

Elements of the forward fire-control tower and the upper parts of the superstructure, mainmast, and smokestack are observed from the same vantage point as in the preceding photograph. At the lower left, above the pilothouse, is the top of the conning tower: a heavily armored structure that contains stations for conning the ship and controlling the gun batteries during battle. A small platform for a searchlight is above the secondary conning bridge on the front of the forward fire-control tower.

A steam whistle and platform are located on each side of the forward fire-control tower, just below the secondary conning bridge. This photo shows the one on the port side of the tower, along with the catwalk and handrail below it. The whistle is a Leslie Tyfon.

A steam whistle of a different type is mounted on the starboard side of the conning tower, below the secondary conning bridge.

The port steam whistle is viewed from the lower front, with the forward port corner of the conning tower to the left.

Inscribed, "USS ALABAMA 1942," the ship's bell is mounted on the front of the forward conning tower. Support braces for the secondary conning bridge are at the top of the photo.

The top of the conning tower is viewed from the level atop the pilothouse. A very heavy steel door is on the thickly armored tower. Inside this level of the conning tower was the fire-control station. On the roof are periscope heads and an antenna for the Mk. 27 radar system, a part of the primary battery's fire-control system that was installed in early 1945. To the left are the forward Mk. 37 director and its foundation.

The forward, or number 1, Mk. 37 secondary-battery director is to the front of the forward fire-control tower. A sheet-metal structure on each side of the director was installed when the ship entered long-term storage after World War II, to protect the optical rangefinder. Three hatches on the upper front of the director were provided for three of the crewmen: the director officer, the pointer, and the trainer. Three more crewmen were located in the rear part of the director.

As seen from above and to the rear, the forward Mk. 37 director has two hatches on the rear of the roof. The large box on the center rear of the director contains the radar transmitter-receiver. Atop the director are the Mk. 12 and Mk. 22 fire-control radar antennas.

The *Alabama*'s superstructure as seen from the port side of turret number one. Above and aft of turret two is the navigating bridge, containing the ship's primary conning station. The front of the navigating bridge is enclosed, and the rear of it is open, with a windshield to deflect air from personnel on that part of the bridge. Below that bridge is the flag bridge, with portholes on its side. Above the navigating bridge is the top of the conning tower, with three vision slits visible on it.

A photo taken from the secondary conning station on the front of the forward fire-control tower shows the top of the conning tower (*foreground*), with the antenna for the Mk. 27 radar and five periscope heads. Farther forward are turrets 1 and 2 and the forecastle. The wooden part of the main deck ends at the breakwater and is made of steel plate from that point forward. Five 20 mm guns, with splinter shields, are on each side of the forecastle.

Twin 5-inch/38-caliber dual-purpose gun mount number 2, the forward mount of that type on the port side of *Alabama*, is viewed from above, with the open part of the flag bridge to the left. Below and forward is a quadruple 40 mm gun mount.

Twin 5-inch/38-caliber gun mounts numbers 1 (*right*) and 3 (*center*) are viewed from the port side of the superstructure. On the sides of the shields are hoods for telescopes, as follow: left front, pointer; left rear, checker (present only during training or practice exercises, to check the fire of the pointer and the trainer); and, *right*, trainer.

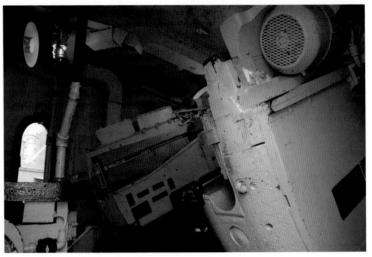

In a view taken through the right side door of a twin 5-inch/38-caliber gun mount, the housings for the two guns are at the center and the left. The housing provided the support structure for the gun and rammer and included the breech mechanism, the slide, firing and casing-ejection systems, and recoil and counterrecoil mechanisms. To the left are the mount captain's platform, painted dark red, and, above it, its support stanchions.

Two side doors for crew access are on the shield of each twin 5-inch/38-caliber gun mount. This is the left one. Two ladder rungs are below it. Toward the bottom of the shield is the left spent-casing port, with its door open.

On the upper right of the housing of the right 5-inch/38-caliber gun, the barrel-shaped mechanism is the hydraulic motor for the rammer, which is to the immediate front of the motor. To the lower right is equipment of the training gear, to the front of which is the trainer's station.

The right gun of the 5-inch/38-caliber dual-purpose gun mount is viewed from the center of the gunhouse, showing the rammer and its hydraulic motor atop the right side of the housing. To the left are the two projectile hoists, in which 5-inch projectiles arrived in the gunhouse from the ammunition-handling compartments below.

In the foreground is the housing of the left 5-inch/38-caliber gun, with the rammer and its motor at the upper left. At the rear of the yellowish part of the housing of the right gun is a vertical object, which is the shell guard, the part of the rammer that made contact with the rear of the shells and projectiles, to push them forward into the breech. The projectiles for these guns weighed 57 pounds, and the powder charges weighed 38 pounds.

The left 5-inch/38-caliber gun and the two projectile hoists are depicted. Visible between the projectile hoists is the forward part of the gunhouse, in which the sight setter and the fuse setter were stationed.

In the left front of the shield of the 5-inch/38-caliber gun mount are the pointer's and the sight checker's stations. The crew inside the cramped confines of the gunhouse totaled thirteen, or fourteen when a sight checker was present. Nine men alone were stationed in the space between the two guns.

On the third deck are the lower powder- and projectile-handling rooms. There, handlers received projectiles and powder charges from adjacent magazines and placed them in the hoists—separate ones for projectiles and powder—several of which are seen here. These hoists transported the ammunition to the upper projectile- and powder- handling rooms, where handlers transferred the ammo to the upper hoists for transfer to the 5-inch/38-caliber gun mounts directly above. *Battleship USS Alabama Memorial Park*

This lower powder- and projectile-handling room contained hoists for sending ammunition up to twin 5-inch/38-caliber gun mounts numbers 1 and 3, the first two such mounts on the starboard side of the superstructure. Inside the door at the center of the photo are several 5-inch projectiles and stacks of the aluminum canisters the powder charges were stored in. To the left is an ammunition hoist. *Battleship USS Alabama Memorial Park*

In a view of the left side of a 5-inch/38-caliber gun mount, the hood for the sight checker's telescope is above and aft of the hood for the pointer's telescope. Toward the lower front of the side of the shield is an access door for components of the gun-elevation mechanism. Below the gunhouse is the drum-shaped barbette.

Six ladder rungs, the trainer's telescope hood, and an access door for the training gear are on the right side of the gunhouse.

Twin 5-inch/38-caliber gun mount number 2 is viewed from above, with the other four twin 5-inch mounts on the port side of *Alabama* also in view. A 24-inch signal-searchlight is on a platform adjacent to mount number 1, on the flag bridge.

The right side of the 24-inch signal-searchlight that appears in the preceding photo is seen from above on its cradle and pedestal.

The dome glass is missing from the front of the 24-inch signal-searchlight, permitting a clear view of the shutters. Around the inside of the drum is the iris shutter, which operated somewhat like the aperture of a camera and could be completely closed, to keep the drum light-tight while the arc lamp was in operation. The small handwheel on the front of the drum operated the iris shutter. Inside the drum is the signal shutter, consisting of sector vanes that operated at high speed to open and shut.

The same 24-inch signal-searchlight is viewed from the front, facing aft on the port side of the flag bridge. To the left are stanchions that support a platform above for a quadruple 40 mm gun mount.

The 24-inch signal-searchlight on the port side of the flag bridge is viewed from its right side.

The quadruple 40 mm antiaircraft gun mount on the forward end of the port side of the first superstructure deck is viewed from above. A clear view is available of the loaders' platforms. Curved metal chutes below the guns served to direct spent cartridge cases forward; the front ends of the four chutes are visible below the rear ends of the gun barrels.

Number of Light Antiaircraft Armament Mounts Aboard USS *Alabama*			
Date	40 mm Quad	20 mm Single	20 mm Twin
August 1942	6	12	–
January 1943	8	35	–
March 1943	12	40	–
May 1943	12	52	–
February 1945	12	52	16
November 1945	14	32	16

Turret 2 on battleship *Alabama* is viewed from the port side. Three 16-inch/45-caliber Mk. 6 guns protrude from the front of the gunhouse. On the rear of the roof is a quadruple 40 mm gun mount on a raised platform surrounded by a splinter shield. Farther forward on the turret roof is a mount for the Mk. 51 director associated with the turret-top 40 mm gun mount. On the side of the gunhouse below the 40 mm mount is the left hood of the rangefinder. Hoods for the trainer's sight (*forward*) and pointer's sight (*rear*) are on the side of the gunhouse below the Mk. 51 director pedestal.

The quadruple 40 mm antiaircraft gun mount above the rear of the roof of turret number 2 is viewed from above. Some of the equipment of this mount is missing, including the pointer's and trainer's seats and ring sights, and the spent-casing chutes.

As viewed from the 40 mm gun mount atop turret 2, a pedestal and cradle for a Mk. 51 director are on the roof of the turret. During World War II, there was a splinter shield around this director; subsequently it was removed. At the top of the photo is the rear of the roof of turret number 1.

This and the next two photos depict a battery of three 20 mm antiaircraft gun mounts on the port side of the main deck, adjacent to the forward part of the superstructure. Shown here is the aft gun mount, a single 20 mm gun with the ammunition magazine attached. On the outboard side of this three-gun battery is a splinter shield, the aft terminus of which is to the left.

The forward gun mount in the three-gun battery shown in the two preceding photos is a Mk. 24 twin 20 mm gun mount. The unique cam stop below the left side of the gun carriage distinguishes this as a Mk. 24. Although the Mk. 24 twin 20 mm gun mounts were authorized for installation on South Dakota–class battleships in 1945, including eight on *Alabama*, a May 1945 report on the ship's ordnance makes it clear that the 20 mm guns on board totaled fifty-six Mk. 4 single mounts. This likely did not change, at least not during the duration of the war.

The middle 20 mm gun mount and its pedestal and shield are positioned inboard of the splinter shield. This mount and the one in the preceding photo are missing the shoulder rests normally installed on the gun carriages. Along the edge of the main deck are a bitt, *left*, for securing a mooring hawser, and a 24-inch closed chock, a fitting for leading out a hawser.

Adjacent to the forward superstructure on the starboard side of the main deck, and just aft of a battery of three 20 mm gun mounts, is a cable reel on a stand. On the deck, forward of turret number 1, is the breakwater, with triangular frames braces on its rear.

The three 20 mm gun mounts next to the forward starboard corner of the superstructure are shown facing aft. The closest piece is an example of a Mk. 24 twin 20 mm gun mount, which was emplaced on some US Navy ships in the final months of World War II.

A single 20 mm gun mount is in the foreground of this photo of the same three-gun battery. During World War II, the 20 mm guns were on Mk. 4 mounts, which were a pedestal type with a handwheel for elevating or depressing the gun and its carriage. These tripod mounts are postwar or postrestoration installations.

A view aft from the forecastle of *Alabama* includes two batteries of three 20 mm guns; the anchor chains and the wildcats, the capstan heads that propel the chains; the breakwater; and turrets 1 and 2 and the superstructure. In the left foreground are the receiver, magazine, and cradle of another 20 mm gun.

A twin 20 mm gun mount on the starboard forecastle faces out toward Mobile Bay. On top of the receivers are two magazines with a capacity of sixty rounds. A handle on the rear of the magazine assisted the loader in lifting it. The gun trigger is on the left handlebar.

The forward starboard 20 mm gun mount on the forecastle is shown behind its splinter shield. The shield and its mount are improvised.

A single 20 mm gun mount features grips on the sides of the receiver. The tripod stand is attached to a steel baseplate with sides contoured to fit level on the forecastle. The original 20 mm gun pedestals were mounted on these round plates.

A close-up of the left side of turret 1 shows, *from front to rear*, the hood for the trainer's telescope, the hood for the pointer's telescope, and the large hood for the left side of the optical rangefinder. These sights, along with an auxiliary fire-control computer, were used when the turret was under local control, rather than under the control of a Mk. 38 primary-battery director. The fronts of the first two hoods have doors on their inboard sides, shown open here. The opening on the front of the rangefinder hood was equipped with a shutter. The same combination of sight hoods is on the right side of the turret.

A view from inside the turret officer's booth faces to the left, with the rangefinder to the left and the inside of the left rangefinder hood lit up on the far end of the rangefinder. To the right is the left side of the transverse bulkhead separating the turret officer's booth from the gun chambers. This bulkhead was sealed to exclude flames and gas from the turret officer's booth. The feature running from left to right along the lower part of the photo is the chain casing for the rammer for the left gun. On the transverse bulkhead to the right of center are red-painted switchboards, and a porthole and door to the left gun chamber.

The left objective of the rangefinder of one of *Alabama*'s turrets is viewed as it is situated inside its armored hood. The photo was taken from within the turret officer's booth in the rear of the turret.

The rangefinder operator sat to the rear of the central part of the rangefinder in the rear of the turret officer's booth. He faced a recessed panel with the main eyepieces. A cushioned pad is above the eyepieces.

The turret officer's booth is viewed toward the left, with the transverse bulkhead to the left, the turret officer's gray-and-yellow-painted periscope to the upper center, and the auxiliary fire-control computer to the lower right. The booth is painted glossy white or a very light gray, except for the floor, which is painted dark red, with nonslip panels attached to it. Some controls and electrical panels are painted red.

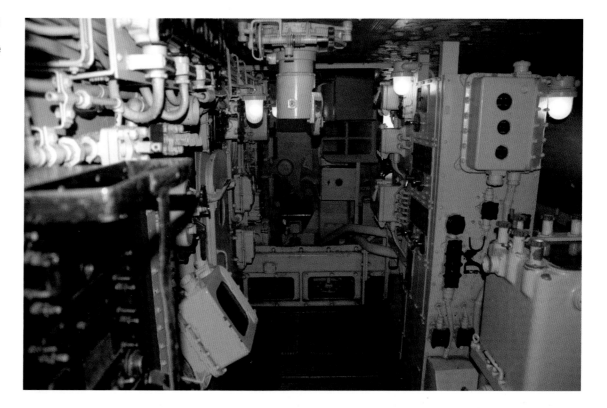

Another photo from the center of the turret officer's booth shows more of the auxiliary fire-control computer, toward the lower left. To the right is the front of the rangefinder. The turret roof has a ridged texture, with the closely spaced ridges running fore and aft.

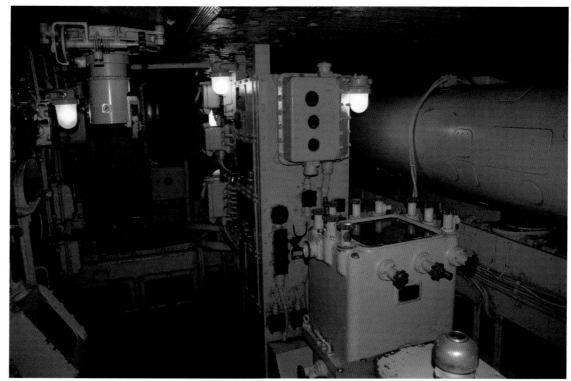

Blast bags, also called bloomers, are fitted to the fronts of the turrets and the barrels of the 16-inch guns, to seal off the opening for the guns. To the lower right is a memorial plaque to crewmen who died in the line of duty.

A 16-inch/45-caliber gun breech and the recoil cylinder (*right*) and counterrecoil cylinder (*left*) are viewed from the upper rear in the tight confines of a gun chamber. At the bottom is the open breech plug; the round inner surface of the plug, facing the camera, is nicknamed the "mushroom."

The same 16-inch/45-caliber gun breech and cylinders are seen from above, with the breech plug in view. Below the plug is the gun pan, the next level below the gunhouse.

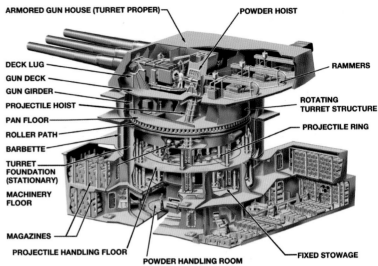

ARMORED GUN HOUSE (TURRET PROPER) — POWDER HOIST

DECK LUG
GUN DECK
GUN GIRDER
PROJECTILE HOIST
PAN FLOOR
ROLLER PATH
BARBETTE

RAMMERS
ROTATING TURRET STRUCTURE
PROJECTILE RING

TURRET FOUNDATION (STATIONARY)

MACHINERY FLOOR

MAGAZINES

PROJECTILE HANDLING FLOOR

POWDER HANDLING ROOM

FIXED STOWAGE

The main battery of any battleship was its principal asset and reason for existing. This diagram of a US Navy three-gun, 16-inch turret provides an idea of its extensive structure, which extended far belowdecks. The gunhouse and the pan floor below it rotated as a unit on rollers on a ring around the inside of the heavily armored barbette. Below that level was the projectile-handling floor, from which stored projectiles were hoisted up to the guns. On the lowest level was the powder-handling room, where powder charges were received from magazines and hoisted up to the guns. Magazines for securely storing ammunition were adjacent to the lower levels of the turret.

In the rear of one of the gun chambers is a cradle, in the raised position. The part of the cradle closest to the camera is the spanning tray, which is hinged to the top of the cradle. Projectiles come up to the gunhouse via a hoist, coming to rest in the raised cradle. To load the gun, the cradle is lowered and the spanning tray extends to the gun breech. Then the projectile is rammed into the gun chamber. Powder bags arrive six at a time on a car through their own trunks, from the magazines and powder-handling rooms far belowdecks to the upper powder-hoist door, *at the lower left*.

Number of Light Antiaircraft Armament Mounts aboard USS *Alabama*			
Date	40 mm Quad	20 mm Single	20 mm Twin
August 1942	6	12	–
January 1943	8	35	–
March 1943	12	40	–
May 1943	12	52	–
February 1945	12	52	16
November 1945	14	32	16

The powder-handling floor of one of *Alabama*'s 16-inch/45-caliber turrets is viewed from above. On the circular bulkhead, to the right of center, two of the six powder-passing scuttles are visible. These provided a safe means of transferring powder bags from the magazine outside the turret, into the powder-handling floor. From these scuttles, powder handlers carried the powder charges to the powder hoists, which are seen to the lower left and the center. The hoists rotated in unison with the turret. To the left is the central column of the turret, with ladder rungs and a black stripe painted on it. *Battleship USS Alabama Memorial Park*

One of the powder hoists, *left*, and one of the powder scuttles, *center*, are in view. There were three powder hoists, serving the three guns in the turret. The hoists were arranged in two groups: a single one and a double one. Six powder bags constituted one powder charge for a gun. *Battleship USS Alabama Memorial Park*

Compartment B-301-C, on the third deck just aft of the barbette of turret number 2, is a control station, containing a switchboard, as seen here; the forward of two master gyrocompasses, partially visible to the lower left; and a control panel and an auxiliary conning station.

The same master gyrocompass is in the right foreground, with the auxiliary conning station in the center background. The master gyrocompass supplied the ship's true compass heading to repeater compasses at numerous other stations around the ship.

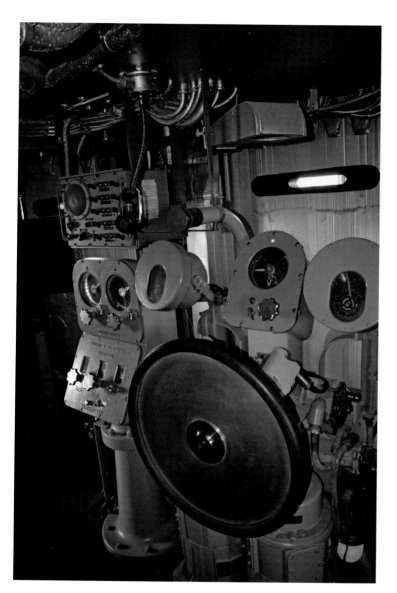

The charthouse, directly aft of the pilothouse, includes desks with drawers for nautical charts, as well as communications equipment. This area underwent restoration around 2016.

The primary conning station, also referred to as the battle bridge or the pilothouse, is in the conning tower at the navigating-bridge level. A vision slit is in the 16-inch-thick armor to the front of the station. Above the steering wheel is the rudder-angle indicator, to the right of which is a compass repeater. To the left of the wheel are the engine-order and engine-revolution indicators and transmitter, above which is an intercom box.

The charthouse is viewed from a point closer to the desk to the right in the preceding photo, facing the door. To the left is a facet of the director trunk, a tube extending from the base of the forward Mk. 37 secondary director down to the flag-bridge level, one level below the charthouse.

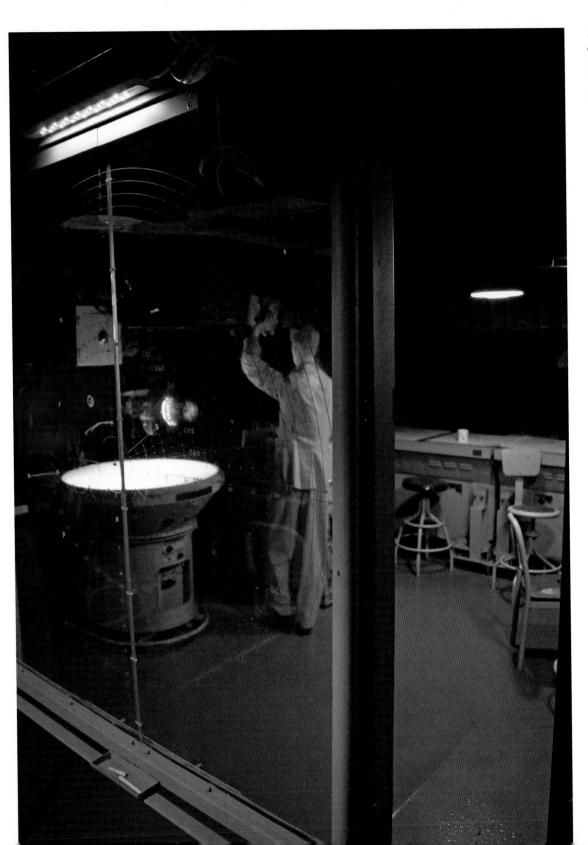

Amidships on the third deck of *Alabama* is the Combat Information Center (CIC), with a mannequin posed to the right of an illuminated plot. The CIC featured radar equipment, plotting devices, and internal and external communications equipment manned by specially trained personnel. They were tasked with informing the flag and ship commanders onboard, as well as personnel in other friendly ships and aircraft, of the positions and headings of friendly and enemy ships and aircraft in the area. A typical CIC also was responsible for target indication, control of aircraft and small craft in the area, and tracking the ship's location when in proximity to land.

A compartment is furnished with a desk with a typewriter and chair, electrical panels, and a plot (*right*). In the background is another compartment with various indicators on a bulkhead above a desk.

Radar sets are arrayed in a compartment belowdecks. The advent of naval radar during World War II gave the United States Navy an edge over its enemies in the ability to identify, track, and accurately target threats in the air and on the surface.

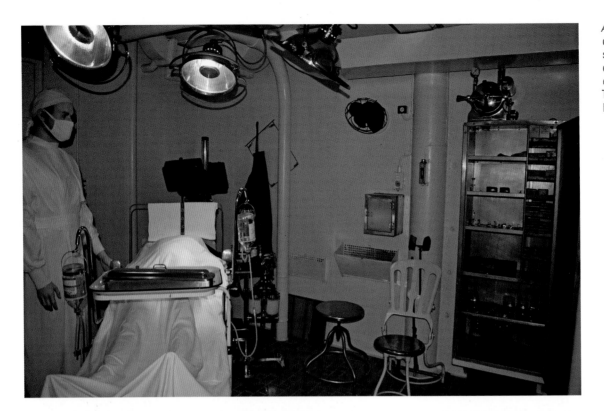

Alabama had a fully equipped operating room, for performing surgeries on battle casualties or on crewmen who were injured or suffering from maladies. The operating room also had x-ray equipment.

Two cots and portable stands and other equipment are shown in the sick bay. Sometimes personnel from smaller ships that lacked operating rooms, x-ray equipment, and other state-of-the-art medical facilities were brought to capital ships such as *Alabama* for treatment.

Alabama had extensive facilities for feeding its approximately 2,500 crewmen and officers. Shown here is a galley, with a stainless-steel sink and table in the foreground and a grill with a mannequin operating behind it.

The ship's butcher shop was equipped with hanging racks, a meat-cutting saw, handsaws, scales, meat-cutting charts, and a butcher block.

The same galley area is viewed from a slightly different position, showing pots and cooking utensils hanging from the overhead.

Warrant officers messed, or ate meals, and spent idle time in this compartment. In the US Navy, a warrant officer is a technical specialist tasked with the proper operation of a specific system or component of the ship. They also train and supervise the technical operators and maintenance men of the battleship.

Alabama's oil-and-water-testing lab was where the ship's supplies of fresh water and fuel and lubricating oils were analyzed on a daily basis. Testing of these fluids was necessary to keep the crew safe and to prevent corrosion to boilers and plumbing.

Alabama's post office was where workers received, sorted, and distributed mail to and from the ship. The announcement of "mail call" over the ship's loudspeakers was cause for celebration and morale-building for the crew.

Packages are stacked on shelves in the post office. The "CENSORED" poster next to the door (the same one shown in the preceding photo) refers to the wartime practice of officers reading the crew's correspondence to censor, with ink, any information that would compromise the security of the ship.

In the photographic lab and darkroom, images generated by the ship's photographers were developed and printed.

Radio central, on the third deck aft of turret 2, was the radio-communications nerve center of *Alabama*. Communications were received and sent over long-range transmitters and receivers. Typists recorded transcripts of all incoming messages, which were received in Morse code. Extensive electrical wiring served the communications equipment.

There are eight Babcock and Wilcox oil-fired boilers deep down in the machinery spaces on *Alabama.* Two boilers are in each of the four machinery spaces. This one is boiler number 2. The boilers generated steam to drive the turbines that propelled the battleship. Evaporators in the ship converted 40,000 gallons of seawater into fresh water for the boilers each day. *Battleship USS Alabama Memorial Park*

The exterior portions of the six burners of boiler number 2 are mounted on octagonal, indented plates. To operate the boilers, the ship carried up to 2.1 million gallons of fuel oil. *Battleship USS Alabama Memorial Park*

Each of the four machinery rooms have, in addition to two boilers, two General Electric turbines, which received steam from the boilers and transmitted power to the reduction gears and the propeller shafts. One high-pressure and one low-pressure boiler was in each machinery room. *Battleship USS Alabama Memorial Park*

The low-pressure steam turbine in machinery room number 1 is displayed. Steam from the boilers first went through the high-pressure turbine; as that steam dissipated in the high-pressure turbine, it was then vented to the low-pressure turbine. In that way, the most economical use was made of the steam. *Battleship USS Alabama Memorial Park*

One of the two five-bladed propellers originally installed on the USS *Alabama* is displayed in the memorial park. The five-bladed propellers were on the outboard shafts, and four-bladed propellers were mounted on the inner shafts. The propellers were removed before the ship departed from Bremerton, Washington, in 1964, and were transported to Mobile on the ship's forecastle.